MW00939803

Gal

I hope i gives you gre insight.

1 Peter 4:11

Just Middle Manager Next Great Leader

Expanding the Range of Your Leadership Style

DAVID J. HULINGS

This is a work of fiction. All of the characters, names, incidents, organizations, and dialogue in this novel are either the products of the author's imagination or are used fictitiously.

WestBow Press books may be ordered through booksellers or by contacting:

WestBow Press
A Division of Thomas Nelson & Zondervan
1663 Liberty Drive
Bloomington, IN 47403
www.westbowpress.com
1 (866) 928-1240

ISBN: 978-1-5127-8585-2 (sc)
ISBN: 978-1-5127-8584-5 (e)

Library of Congress Control Number: 2017906511

Print information available on the last page.

WestBow Press rev. date: 05/22/2017

Thanks and Dedication

Several years ago my new wife, Robin, and I merged our families. Her three children and my four (along with a new son-in-law and a beautiful granddaughter) moved into a three-bedroom ranch home with one bathroom. The first year was tough.

With the possibility of a second divorce right around the corner, we had to do something. We determined we had to discover what made our children tick and adapt our parenting and leadership skills to their appetites for life, not according to our own. By doing so, not only did we save our marriage and raise seven wonderful children, we also discovered that each of the seven had a different appetite for life. To adjust to all seven appetites, our parenting learning curve was longer and much more difficult, but it was also much more productive and rewarding.

During the last fifteen years, our children and my wife have taught me much about leadership and the varying appetites of individuals. It is to my family and my wife I say thanks. Without your love, support, and patience, this work would not be possible.

I dedicate the pages of this book, however, to the one who taught me from his book more about leadership and about the unique appetites we each hold than all the books ever written on leadership combined. God, through the pages of the Holy Scripture, has led me on a wonderful journey through life, guiding me to many truths about leaders and leadership via his Word. I dedicate this book to his glory.

> If any man speaks, he should do it as one speaking the very words of God. If anyone serves, he should do it with the strength God provides, so that in all things God may be praised through Jesus Christ. To him be the glory and the power for ever and ever. Amen.
>
> 1 Peter 4:11

Contents

Part III: Conclusion

Foreword

While rich and powerful in the insights they can provide, the archetypes leave so many with a powerful question—Okay, so now what? How do I move from awareness to action? In this fable, David Hulings has given us more than just an interesting read, he has given us a road map to understand ourselves and the challenges we all have in nurturing the leader that sleeps within us.

Hile Rutledge
Chief Executive Officer
OKA (Otto Kroeger Associates)

Preface

Just Middle Manager is everyone who has ever desired to become a better leader, the Next Great Leader, of their organization, institution, or business. To become the Next Great Leader, your ability to identify and apply the proper leadership style at the appropriate time is imperative for success. In these pages, you will be introduced to twelve leadership styles based upon Carl Jung's archetypes, learning about both the strengths and the shadowy sides of each archetype.

To understand the concepts of an archetype, think about the person behind Superman, Clark Kent; which one is he? Is he really Superman, or is he really Clark Kent? (It probably depends on if he is wearing spandex or not!) What, if any, are the strengths and/or shadows of either one?

Superman and Clark Kent are the same person but with two different ways to project that person. Similarly, an archetype is a way we project and portray ourselves. If we were to describe our personalities as the hardware of our lives, archetypes would be the software. You might have only one hardware set of preferences, but you can run multiple software programs. Those software programs are our archetypes. You might have the same personality as someone else but might look and act totally different because you are acting out *different archetypes.* One might look like Superman, and the other might look like Clark Kent.

The author has tried to present each archetype in both their strengths and shadows. However, since there remains much to be written on each archetype, it could appear as though more has been omitted in this book than could be recorded. The book is meant to be an *introduction* into the journey of the leader via the archetypes. It is not meant to be a textbook describing every nuance of each archetype.

Also, please note that even though Just Middle Manager is referred to as a male in the book, the reader should not believe that there is a male-oriented over female-oriented view of leadership found within the pages. The leadership journey is as equally challenging and profitable for a male or a female traveler should they take the necessary steps to follow that dream and vision.

To all who read, enjoy your journey. The reward at the end of the path is not only bountiful but also beneficial.

Prologue

Roy slammed the small sedan's transmission into park and jumped out of the car, leaving the thin manila envelope on the passenger seat beside him.

"Jill, Jill," he yelled as he pushed open the door, bursting into the foyer of their modest two-bedroom city home. It was the first home they had purchased together, right after their marriage. They had commented many times about how quaint it was, but today, it looked very small. By the time he heard Jill respond from the basement, Roy was already envisioning their future four-bedroom, split-level home in the country. As he bounded down the steps to their make-shift laundry room, he was already dreaming of a country home with enough land for a small garden and a large dog.

"I got it, honey; I got it," Roy exclaimed, grabbing her around the waist, lifting and swinging her around like a rag doll.

"You got it? It's official?" Jill asked, not bothering to inquire what "it" was, knowing full well what Roy was so excited about.

"Well, I still have to meet with the leadership team tomorrow, but Sandy said that should just be a formality. She says it's a *done deal,*" Roy answered. "I think they want to see if I am really leadership material. But Sandy said she would give them a great recommendation. I guess Jim is a little worried, but he's always worried. He is always looking for cliffs on the path that others aren't," Roy added, setting Jill down on top of the dryer. It didn't matter to him that by doing so he knocked a pile of clothes Jill had just folded onto the floor.

"Roy!" Jill shouted as she wiggled off the dryer and tried to bend over to pick up the freshly creased shirts. "What is Jim worried about?" she added, refolding Roy's old Harley T-shirt. "If it is a 'done deal,' what more do you have to do? You've already been interviewed four times. It's just a higher leadership position. How much more do you have to prove to them? You are already one of the best middle managers they have."

"That's just it, Jill, I'm *just a middle manager.* I want to be more. I want to be the Next Great Leader there," he said making a veiled attempt to help refold the misplaced laundry.

"You know what I mean," Jill said, ignoring his help and refolding the clothes he had just folded. "If it is a done deal, what is Jim worried about then?" she asked again.

After a moment of thinking, he responded to Jill's question, saying, "I think Jim is worried because when he met with the leadership team prior to his promotion, he didn't fair too well. He said they only asked him one question, but he froze when he tried to answer."

"What was the question?" Jill asked, placing the laundry into the torn hamper. She handed the full basket to Roy and headed back up stairs.

"Oh my gosh! Wait until you see! But I left it in the car! I'll be right back!" Roy answered racing up the stairs behind her, hamper in hand. Dropping the hamper at the front door, he retreated to the tan and white sedan he left in the driveway. He had to retrieve that small, manila envelope (unless he wanted to stumble like Jim did in his final interview). *What else will I have to prove in order to become the next leader at Brisco Chemical Exchange,* he asked himself.

Part I:

Discovering an Appetite

The Big Question

"You left what in the car?" Jill asked from the kitchen, opening the refrigerator door. "Hey! What do you want for dinner tonight?" she yelled, before noticing Roy had already returned from his trip to the car and was standing right behind her. Jill asked the question as though she were on a mission of her own. "I am not sure what I'm hungry for," she said, answering her own question and not waiting for Roy's response. "I just can't get a grip on my appetite," she added with a smile, moving from the refrigerator and taking a step past Roy to the door of the pantry.

Roy smiled back, knowing full well why her appetite had been so radical these last few months. Envelope in hand, he walked up behind her and reached around her small waist to softly pat her slightly bulging stomach. "You better eat something," he said. "You're eating for two, now, you know."

"Yes, I know," Jill said, "but I just can't get my exotic appetite to agree with what we have in our mundane pantry. What's that?" she asked, pulling her head out of the pantry and noticing for the first time the envelope in Roy's right hand.

"This is the cheat-sheet for tomorrow morning's interview," Roy stated, looking up just in time to watch Jill stick a piece of a Hershey's chocolate bar into her mouth.

"It's not really a cheat-sheet actually. That's what Jim called it," he added. "It's the agenda for tomorrow. The interview committee told Jim to give it to me. It gives me the names of the twelve people on the leadership team that will be conducting the final interview.

And it says I will be asked only one question and given just ten minutes to complete my answer."

"What's the question? Who's on the interview team?" Jill asked, putting the Hershey's wrapper into her pocket like a child trying to hide something from her parents.

"The twelve members of the leadership team are from the Executive Leadership Board. The interview team changes for each interview, but the question is the same question Jim and Sandy had to answer. Jim said he froze when he was asked. They actually told him to come back a month later, after he thought about his answer. He really struggled with it at first. He said that month was a real journey for him. But eventually, obviously, they promoted him as a new leader. He said he lost sleep over trying to get just the right answer."

"Well, what's the question?" Jill asked, ignoring her appetite for the moment and taking the single, white sheet of paper out of the envelope.

The typing on the paper was double-spaced, and the title was in a larger font than the rest of the information on the page. It was printed on official Brisco Chemical Exchange stock white paper. The title across the top was in two lines and read, "Final Interview: Roy Weatherspoon (9:00 a.m. to 9:10 a.m., June 6)." Under the title were the words "Interview Committee." It contained twelve names in alphabetical order. Jill only knew a few of the names on the list but knew they were very high up in the Brisco Chemical Exchange world. The name Harvey Brisco, the co-founder and owner of Brisco, was listed first.

"Mr. Brisco, himself, is on the interview team?" Jill asked.

"Apparently," Roy responded, trying to read the instructions over Jill's shoulder. He could see someone from each of the twelve departments at Brisco. He didn't know any of them very well, however, only except by reputation. Under the list of names, was a single question that read, "What is your leadership style, and how would it benefit Brisco Chemical Exchange?"

Jill continued to look over the names and read them out loud until she noticed that Roy had turned around and was staring out the kitchen window. She knew Roy's quiet, "lead-from-behind" approach made him less confident than most people who had "natural-lead-from-the-front" leadership skills. It took Jill three months to convince him to apply for this leadership position.

But like all those times during her prompting, Roy had once again teleported himself to some other place and time. It was a place where he questioned not only his ability to lead, but his desire to lead, as well.

> Insight: Society, the business world, and almost all organizations tend to place more value on those who lead from the front than they do on those who lead from behind. Leading from behind is a great art that most leaders must eventually learn. However, it comes with an apparent risk that others may believe you are not a "natural" leader. To lead from behind is simply another form of leadership that is not always positively recognized by others, nor promoted within organizations. When leading from behind, you may actually be the hand in the sock puppet or on the other end of the strings of the marionette, but if others can't see you, they don't always believe you are leading.

Jill walked up beside him and slid her hand onto his shoulder. "Roy, you can't worry about this now!" she exclaimed. "You have made it through all these other interviews and, apparently, knocked others out of the running. This is just one more question to answer. What are you worried about?" she asked, rotating him away from the window to look him in the eyes for the first time since he had arrived home. "This seems to be a pretty easy question to answer," she added, turning away after a long kiss on his lips.

For a moment, Roy forgot his leadership journey and envisioned a passage of romance. But for Jill, this romantic interlude was brief, at best. Over the past few months the urges of her stomach had more desire than that of her libido. At this stage of her pregnancy, Jill would rather have a great meal than a great time. Once again she began looking through the cupboards for something that would satisfy her appetite. Roy was left with a passionate fantasy of mere crumbs.

"You think this question should be easy to answer?" he asked, sarcastically, turning his mind back to leadership and Jill's insinuation that his interview would be simple. "Will it be as easy as you finding something that can satisfy your hunger and is more nutritious for our child than a Hershey Bar?" Roy asked, the corner of his lips turning up into his patented *I-caught-you* smile.

"Yeah, that's easy," Jill said, ignoring him, taking the remaining dark chocolate out of her sweater pocket, placing a large piece into her mouth, and staring at him with her patented, *I-will-eat-what-I-want,* rebellious look.

"Well, let's see who gets the answer first," Roy said, ignoring her sassy attitude. "Let's see if you can discover what will satisfy your appetite for food before I can solve my *appetite* for leadership style."

"*Appetite,* I like that. Very clever, for you," Jill said, again, clearly sarcastically. "And, that's a bet I'll probably lose but would love to try to win," Jill said with a smile. "I guess I'll just have to *force myself* to eat everything I find in order to discover what I'm actually hungry for," she added, the smirk on her face turning to a full-blown smile.

"I doubt if I'll have that much enjoyment," Roy said, staring down at the names on the paper he was now holding. "From what I know about these twelve leaders, they each have a different form of leadership. If I give an answer tomorrow to please one of them, one of the others may not agree. No wonder Jim had such a tough time."

Insight: Each of us has a way we want to live our lives. It is the *type* of way we feel comfortable living. It can be characterized as our *appetite* for life. Our appetite can consist of many things, not the least of which is our personality type, our core values, the life story we are living, and many other key ingredients. If we can discover our appetite for life, we can more readily discover our appetite for leadership.

Roy left Jill to her journey through the pantry and went into their modest living room. He sat down in his favorite chair and began to muse about what leadership was all about and what his own leadership style might look like. The only thing he knew was that he didn't want to be *just a middle manager*. Roy wanted to be the *Next Great Leader* at Brisco Chemical Exchange.

As he sat thinking in the chair, Roy had no clue what would solve Jill's hunger. But he thought he ought to know his own appetite for leadership. It shouldn't be that hard.

He could hear Jill pilfering through the pantry looking to solve her hunger pangs. Roy knew she would come across more relatives of Mr. Hershey, as well as Miss Twinkie, Master Potato Chip, and a little help from Captain Crunch. He smiled briefly and then once again looked at the twelve names on his sheet. The smile left quicker than it appeared.

Jill has all those options, but who will help me solve my appetite for leadership? he asked himself. In his stressed state, however, Roy didn't realize that the journey he was about to embark upon would provide him with twelve leadership styles he could use to answer Mr. Brisco's simple question.

What Will Satisfy Your Leadership Hunger?

By the time Jill had finished in the bathroom, Roy was already in bed, still holding his legal pad; the top sheet was still blank, as it had been for the entire evening.

"Well, how are you doing? You've been working on that all night," Jill said, looking at Roy's pad of paper as she crawled into bed. She was being very careful not to spill a tuna fish sandwich off the paper plate she had firmly gripped in her hand.

"I'm having about as much luck as you are with your project," Roy answered, covering his nose (the tuna smell was fully permeating their bedroom). "Let's see: a full plate of spaghetti; garlic bread topped with peanut butter, asparagus, and crackers covered with pickles and cheese; popcorn mixed with M & Ms; and now a smelly tuna fish sandwich ... on rye bread. Have you figured out your appetite woes with all that consumption?" Roy asked. He was enjoying reviewing Jill's evening menu selections if only to get his mind off the lack of progress on his own menu for leadership.

"Well, everything I ate tonight, including this sandwich, provided an answer to my appetite question. I was hungry for all of them," Jill said with a big smile, carefully eating away at the tuna and rye; she suddenly wished she had another pickle to add to the flavor.

"Maybe that's the answer for your *blank* piece of paper," she said, emphasizing *blank* for special affect. "You've been searching all night for that *one* answer to your question; that *one* leadership style that is all yours—your appetite—as you put it. But, maybe your appetite is made up of more than just one thing. Maybe you have something that is a combination of garlic, asparagus, popcorn, and tuna?"

"Let's hope not," Roy said, still covering his nose as he laid his yellow pad on the night stand, and turning off his lamp in the process.

Jill ignored his jabs and finished her sandwich. Actually, she thought she had a great idea. Maybe Roy was too worried about identifying that one leadership style everyone was suppose to have, when, in reality, he was a mixture of many good types of styles. Maybe that is what gave Roy (and everyone else for that matter) his own unique appetite for leadership. But, what did she know? She did know one thing: The mixture of garlic and tuna did have a unique aroma.

Insight: There seems to be an overriding theme when we read leadership books that we, as both young and mature leaders, are suppose to fall into some special fashion of leadership and are to mimic a prescribed pattern. We tend to want to look at great leaders and emulate their "style." Whereas this might prove to be effective for some, it isn't for many. Since what we actually know about great leaders is limited, we don't really know the full compilation of their appetite, which severely limits our ability to emulate them. Perhaps it might be wiser to determine the assemblage of our own appetites and then attempt to assimilate their qualities into our own styles. That not only gives a greater chance of performance success, but it also allows us to be true to ourselves. Discover your own appetite before inputting the appetite of others into your leadership style.

As Jill placed the empty plate on her nightstand and reached for the light switch on her side of the bed, she asked Roy, "Did you take your pills tonight, honey?"

"Yes," Roy answered, already starting to doze off. "But, I think I am going to quit taking them. Ever since the doctor prescribed them, I have been tossing and turning every night and have had some wicked nightmares. I'm ready to tell the doctor just what he can do with his pills."

"Doing that would demonstrate a definite leadership style," Jill said sarcastically. "It's called the Foolish and Stubborn Leader! He gave you the pills because he thought they would help. You can't just stop taking them."

"Easy for you to say, at least you can sleep," Roy said, rolling to his back, his mind still racing and thinking about how he would answer his one-question interview.

"Maybe you will dream of your leadership appetite," Jill said, half-joking and half-hoping. She so much wanted Roy to be at peace at nine o'clock the next morning.

"Yeah, I can just hear myself during the interview: 'Well, last night I had this dream about my own individual appetite for leadership, and here is what it taught me—'how do you think that would go over?"

"Well, that depends on what you dream," Jill quipped.

In the darkness, they both laid on the same bed but with different thoughts. Roy was thinking how he would answer the question of his leadership style the next morning. He knew full well he would have a hard time sleeping without an answer. Jill's thoughts were on her menu items for the evening. Would it allow her to sleep at all?

As Roy started to doze off, he realized Jill may have actually been right. Maybe it wasn't one style that defined his leadership. Maybe there was a menu of items that he could choose from that would solve his appetite for leadership. He did hope he would dream of the answer to the question while he slept, because he certainly hadn't come up with anything while he was awake.

As he dozed off, Roy would soon discover Jill was right; he would dream. But would his dream prove to be profitable for his quest or just another one of his nightmares? Was he destined to be just middle manager and never the *Next Great Leader*?

Part II:

The Dream of a Dozen Lessons

The Dream-Journey Begins

Roy was only asleep for an hour or so when his doctor's prescription, his long day, Jill's garlic and tuna odor, and his urgent need to answer the interview question began to take their toll. His tossing and turning were indicative of his mood that entire evening. He couldn't get comfortable in his mind, and the residual affects of that condition weren't appeased by a soft pillow and a warm quilt. He needed answers for the large burden he was carrying. Although his real weight was intellectual, it actually made his back hurt as though he were carrying a heavy pack over his shoulders.

When his dream began, Roy actually thought he was the audience watching the events he was imagining. He knew he was dreaming, but he didn't have the energy to wake up to stop it, nor did he think he wanted to. Like the producer of a movie, he was off-screen while the camera of his mind shot the on-screen scenes of this night time motion picture. From the perch of this evening trance, he could see someone walking up a very winding but narrow path at the beginning of a wonderful valley. He thought the man looked remarkably like himself, but since he could only see the man from behind, he drew no conclusions. The pace of the traveler he observed was slow but steady. The man walked as though he knew where he was going but not really sure why he was going. On the man's back was a very large pack that actually looked more like a burden than possible supplies for his journey. On the side of the pack was a nametag. Roy could barely make out the name, but when he did, he knew why he recognized the man and why he thought it was him. The nametag on the backpack read, *Just Middle Manager.*

In his hand Just Middle Manager held a map. Again, it was tough for Roy to read it through the fog of the dream, but he could see the title at the top of the map. It read, "Directions to Celestial City of Influence for the Next Great Leader." The map looked torn and tattered. The frayed edges exposed that Just Middle Manager had been holding and fretting over his chart for a lengthy amount of time. Yet, by the look of his spirit, Just Middle Manager didn't seem like he was any closer to his destination than the day he had begun. Roy realized when he saw the title of the map that his own intellectual journey was about *influence.* How would he, as a leader, really influence others? What style would he use to persuade those he was leading?

These were just two more questions he added to the burden he already had on his back when he had lain down for the evening. His dream was simply adding to his confusion. The pack on Just Middle Manager's back seemed to grow larger with each of Roy's added questions.

> Insight: Leadership is first and foremost about *influence.* It is about your ability to influence others to accomplish some greater task they wouldn't do naturally on their own and/or work toward a greater good they might not necessarily pursue by themselves. Your ability to get them to accomplish this is based upon your ability to influence them.

The trail Just Middle Manager was traveling was very narrow. It was not wide enough for two to walk side-by-side. It didn't appear to be unsafe, and it was well-traveled. It was just worn enough for Just Middle Manager to know that he was not the only one who had ever walked the path, but it was pure enough for him to think he may have been the only one on the path for a long time. Why was he feeling alone?

Was this another burden of leadership that needed to be learned? Was it possible to travel this journey with others so that the burden was not compounded by loneliness? Again, with each of Roy's questions, Just Middle Manager's pack grew heavier in weight and more awkward in size.

With the added weight in his pack, Just Middle Manager was growing weary with each step that he took. He needed to rest and reflect. Did he really want to travel to Celestial City of Influence? He actually was ready to stop and simply return to where he had started his journey. He was thinking about returning back to the day he was just One of Many in a group, when he wasn't leading but following. There was comfort back there, a false peace for the leading soul, but a peace nonetheless.

Insight: Leadership can be a lonely place. If you are looking to have company in the positions you take as a leader, you may not be really leading: You may just be standing taller and shouting louder than others in the pack. Leadership is about stepping out and having others follow. This concept is called *leadership*. And it can be lonely at times but doesn't have to be. If you are leading and others are following, you ought to have company. But, the strength of your leadership will tell you if it is sooner or later; preferably it will be sooner.

Fortunately, a few yards down the road, there was a large collection of rocks. From within its crevices the formation had a bubbling, natural spring. As Just Middle Manager approached, he could faintly make out someone sitting on top of the structure. Perched high on the rocks and seated so he could see both the winding road forward and the path Just Middle Manager had already traveled, was a figure dressed in a bright robe. It was Leader Innocent. Just Middle Manager didn't realize it, but the cool water he would soon raise to his parched lips would pale in comparison to the refreshment Leader Innocent's spoken words would be for his hungry, leader soul.

Words of Hope and Optimism from Leader Innocent

"Greetings, Traveler! It's a great day to be on a quest, isn't it?" Innocent spoke while looking up to catch the heat from the blazing sun. It was impossible while gathering the heat of the sun for Innocent to notice that Just Middle Manager had already bent his head to drink from the cool spring collecting in the hollow of the rocks below.

"Yes, it is a great day, if you have assurance of both your destiny and of your arrival," Just Middle Manager answered. "I don't have either. So the day is affable for neither travel nor for foolish chatter," he added, not really wanting to talk to anyone. He especially didn't want to converse with someone who appeared to be full of glee when he, himself, was consumed with despondency.

Insight: The appetite of a leader following the style of Leader Innocent sees a great day in everything. They are filled with hope and optimism, despite the gloom and doom of those around them or the circumstances they face. For the Leader Innocent there is a silver lining in every cloud. Leader Innocent might lead with vision and inspiration for what can happen as life's opportunities present themselves. Leader Innocent will inspire and desire those they lead to be positive and always looking on the bright side of the day, rewarding those who are cheerful and optimistic first. At the end of the day Innocent might say it was a great day because everything worked out, just as he or she thought it would, inspiring others to have an equally great outlook despite the tragedy or difficulty they are in.

Leader Innocent ignored Just Middle Manager's gloomy tone and slid down the rocks with energy and excitement. Innocent had been perched on the structure for some time and was absolutely elated to have someone to engage in conversation. It mattered not to Innocent that his subject (this weary traveler) appeared hopeless and dejected.

"Where are you headed that you have no assurance of arrival," Innocent asked, again with eyes toward the sunshine, captured not only by its heat but also by its light.

Just Middle Manager lifted his head from the dark drinking pool, appropriately named the Drinking Pool, but not high enough to catch the rays of the sun. He wiped the water dripping from his chin and answered Innocent in a flat, dispassionate pitch, "I am headed for Celestial City of Influence. It was my original hope at the commencement of my journey to arrive there and to be crowned Next Great Leader."

"Wonderful," Innocent replied. "I have met many a traveler on this path headed for such a place. I hear it is an inviting city for the soul who can reach it. You have chosen your destination well, my friend. What is your name, and perhaps I can travel with you?" Innocent asked, seeing that Just Middle Manager had already finished his refreshment from the Drinking Pool and had returned to the path before him. "My name is Innocent," he added, calling out as Just Middle Manager picked up his pace further down the path.

"My name is Just Middle Manager, and I would prefer to travel alone, if you don't mind ... Innocent," he added, thinking how curious and uncommon the name Innocent must be.

"Well, traveling alone is one way to get to the Celestial City, but traveling light is much quicker," Innocent responded, ignoring the comment that Just Middle Manager wanted to be alone and rather noticing the large pack on his back. "Why do you carry such a load with you? Are those provisions for your journey? Would it help if you had someone who would assist you in carrying them?" Just Middle Manager didn't really want a traveling companion, but the offer for someone to assist in bearing the burden on his back was too much to ignore. He slowed his pace and attempted to lower the pack but had considerable trouble doing so. Each time he tried to lower the load it spun him around in circles. He looked a little like a dog chasing his tail—with as much success.

"It doesn't appear as though the load is meant to be discharged," Innocent said, stating the obvious, which only further frustrated Just Middle Manager. "Perhaps we can seek out someone to assist with this problem that is more familiar with such a quandary? Or, perhaps someone will come along to lift the burden from your back?" Innocent suggested, not really knowing what the real problem was or why Just Middle Manager couldn't release this yoke created by the pack.

Failing to release the burden, Just Middle Manager found rest on a fallen log, which had settled along the path. His attempt to remove the burden from his back, and his journey so far, had taken its toll. He was exhausted.

Just Middle Manager didn't know why he couldn't release the load, but he was sure he wasn't going to try again in the near future. The tussle had taken what little spirit and motivation he had left. He was content to sit on the log for some time.

> Insight: The appetite of Leader Innocent when faced with problems is to find someone to assist with the difficulty they may be facing, while at the same time maintaining hope for a positive outcome. However, Innocent may, at times, hope for aid, without actually ever receiving it. Any hope may, at times, be stronger than the reality of there being any would-be savior. Leader Innocent may only offer the idea that help would be great but not actually offer any help.

"Friend, have you lost your bearings?" Innocent asked, finding a spot on the same log and being careful not to alarm Just Middle Manager. "I detect that the load on your back has placed a heavy hand on your heart as well. Life does not have to be this weighty, my friend. I would imagine the load you feel today will soon be replaced by a brighter hope tomorrow. Your struggle can soon be exchanged for the expectations you have for your future. You are traveling to Celestial City of Influence. You must continue to recall and imagine the wealth of treasure awaiting you upon your arrival.

This thought should give you constant energy and excitement for both your travel, as well as those who may follow you."

"Follow *me*?" Just Middle Manager asked sarcastically. (He did feel a little less fatigued upon hearing the theme of Innocent's words.) "What makes you think that anyone would follow me? I have not only lost my liveliness but also my focus. This is the burden I carry on both back and heart. If I am to become a leader of others, I must be able to direct myself. How could I expect others to follow me when I am so lost on my own? I have discovered that before I can release this burden I must determine my own leadership style and acquire the ability to articulate that style to others. This is what weighs me down and waylays my progress."

Upon hearing Just Middle Manager's dilemma, Innocent bounced to his feet and said, "If it is a particular style you are searching for, I invite you to become the Leader Innocent. It has served me well these many years, and I suspect it will well into the far future." Innocent was eager to share this suggestion, not fully believing that anyone could be as glum and misplaced as Just Middle Manager had presented himself.

Innocent had long been leading others with a quiet, yet buoyant, hope for tomorrow. There were many travelers to Celestial City of Influence that had taken such advice and found their way once again on the right road to a better place. Although there were many a critic who thought Innocent was too Pollyannaish; Innocent thought finding good and seeing hope in all things was an important aspect of any leadership style. While many would think that leading by inspiration and vision of that which is good is, at times, unrealistic, Innocent thought it was not only a good way to view leadership but a pleasant way to be led—for those who are apt to follow. When others were lost in the dullness of their dilemma, Leader Innocent could offer hope for the bleak, a life ring in the sea of suspicion.

"Don't you think that being so ignorant of the conditions at hand is like sticking your head in the proverbial sand? Do you not see this weight I carry?" Just Middle Manager asked. He did not and could not move from the lumber of his log, but once again, he did feel a small lightening of the load as he mused about Innocent's speech concerning the treasures to be found in Celestial City of Influence.

"What makes you believe that I am ignorant of the conditions? Or, that I have stuck my head into the sand?"

"Because," Just Middle Manager said, as he began his answer, "you have neither offered a way for me to release my load nor presented a way to lighten it yourself."

"Perhaps your load, this burden to discover your leadership style, is heavy because you have missed the power of simple hope and the influence of quiet joy that is offered to all leaders who can see the beauty of innocence in all struggles?" Innocent asked. "Have you considered such a thought?"

Just Middle Manager was beginning to understand the meaning behind Leader Innocent's name. But he continued with his argument and asked, "By what reason do I have hope? How can a leader offer hope when there is no real solution to the problem? Although by just talking to you my burden does seem lighter; it is obviously still here, and I sense you are underestimating the difficulty of my state."

"True, there are those who might believe leading by and through the power of innocence is only a camouflage of hope and not true hope, indeed. And, yes, the word *hope,* alone—flying solo—holds little help for those who hold to it. Yet, the hope we hold is never thought of as a single word, but rather the word finds its strength in the context of what we are hoping for or in. The burden on your back and in your heart feels a little less grave because you took a moment to think of the blessings waiting for you in Celestial City of Influence. Consider the runner in a marathon: The runner may lose strength if he or she only listens to the drum beat of their legs as each limb beats out the weight they carry up a sharp incline. Yet, when the runner thinks about the hope of the finish and the rewards of training, he finds his legs much lighter and, often, the slope in front of him much flatter. Their hope is found both in the context of the past (their extensive training) and in the framework of the future (the joy at the finish line). So you see hope is not a camouflage, but the compass pointing toward something practical and real.

"I see your thoughts," Just Middle Manager said as he reflected on Leader Innocent's argument. And, after a brief moment, he added, "If I lose hope as a leader and if I lose the view that things can always work out, I will, in turn, lose my influence over my own motivations. And, if I lose influence over my own self and have little energy and enthusiasm to lead others to safety or to their desired destination, they too will suffer and be de-energized. That hope is not empty but has its basis in the competency of the past and the splendor of what the future holds. Is that what you are saying?"

"Yes, that sums it up very nicely," Innocent answered.

The two sat together on the log for a brief moment with Just Middle Manager eventually joining Leader Innocent's gaze toward the sun to catch its heat and light. Then, breaking the silence between them, Just Middle Manager said, "Certainly a hope, a positive outlook, and a gentle manner of optimism are important to the strength of any leadership style. However," he went on to ask, "isn't there a shadowy side of that manner of leading others? Aren't there pitfalls I should be aware of in your style should I adopt it for my own? Doesn't the shadow of the style hinder its strengths ... its shinier sides?"

"Of course, there are pitfalls. There are pitfalls in any style you may adopt. And, as you continue your journey along this path, you will undoubtedly run into many companions, such as me, who will also offer their styles to you. If you look at each, you may see some shiny sides and some dark shadowy sides in them all. I choose to see their strengths as those things I will adopt. I will consider their shadows as mere opportunities in dirty clothes, which, after cleansing, will become great strengths as well."

"I cannot fault your optimism, for it has, indeed, lightened both the size and the weight of my burden," Just Middle Manager said as he raised himself from the log. "I shall go on to Celestial City of Influence and continue my quest to be named Next Great Leader. Having had our discussion, I now believe that any great leader must have Leader Innocent woven into his or her style. I shall gravitate to your leadership strengths and be aware that the shadows of your style, like the difficulties of life, are but opportunities dressed in filthy rags. I will move forward down this path with a lighter load and a softer burden, not only on my back but in my heart."

With that said, Just Middle Manager looked briefly at his map, gazed toward the sun, and proceeded down the path before him. Only once did he turn to see Leader Innocent, who had already returned to the rock formation and the pool of refreshment awaiting the next weary traveler. It was obvious then to Just Middle Manager that leaders must be able (and be willing) to lead followers, ever so wisely, past a similar Drinking Pool. That is the work and the focus of the Leader Innocent style.

With that thought Just Middle Manager's burden seemed much lighter to carry as he energetically bounded down the path. Yet, he would only be a few steps down the road when this new life philosophy would be challenged and his leadership style further defined. It would be good for his leadership soul, but not good for Roy's sound sleep.

Just Middle Manager was about to meet the antithesis of his newfound friend, Leader Innocent. He was about to meet Leader Orphan.

Insight Tips for putting *Leader Innocent* to work in your own Leadership Style - *Successfully*

1 Begin to look at each problem you face by gathering specific positive outcomes the problem might accomplish. Make a list of positive outcomes in a purely optimistic manner. Of course, those outcomes might not ever be realized. But they certainly won't be realized if you are not looking for them ahead of time.

2 In the darkest hour, remember what you believed. Don't doubt in the dark what you believed in the light. Make a specific list of those things that are true no matter the circumstances you face. Principles you live by are not diminished by circumstances you face; they are simply clouded by the fog of the war you now find yourself fighting.

3 Remember, things don't always work out. Don't be crushed when things don't work out as you thought they might. Sometimes life doesn't have a fairytale ending. It is okay to hurt, and it is okay to have hurt happen when it is out of your control to change it.

4 Don't get caught looking so far into a pleasant future that you get blindsided by the reality of today. You have to pay careful attention to the problems of today, for they won't go away simply because you are looking for a silver lining. The rain doesn't quit simply because you think of the sun.

5 Others won't always bail you out. You may have to solve your own problems with a planned, specific approach. Think about how things should be and then put together a plan that you, personally, will complete to make sure it happens. There may be someone to rescue you, but the rescuer may be waiting for you to do something yourself. The tossed life-ring is only valuable when the drowning victim reaches for its salvation.

Words of Warning and Vulnerability from Leader Orphan

As Just Middle Manager stood, looking at the large canyon before him, he contemplated Leader Innocent's words of hope and of having a positive outlook no matter what one faced in life's journey. But his positive mindset couldn't explain how he had come to the chasm he was now facing. The path he was traveling led him directly to the edge of a very large precipice looking over the vast valley. Although the valley appeared inviting, the overhang was more than unattractive.

Suddenly, with a large amount of sarcasm, a voice behind him said, "Maybe with a lot of *hope* and a lot of *good thoughts* and *optimism,* stairs will suddenly appear, and you can just walk down to the valley floor." The large amount of mockery in the tone of this voice could have filled the gorge that was now facing Just Middle Manager.

Regretfully it wasn't the tone that simply bothered Just Middle Manager. Just as the voice spoke, he happened to be leaning over the edge of the overhang (he was trying to get a better focus on what he was up against should he decide to descend). The voice, although not loud, was piercing enough to startle him and enough to cause him to lose his balance. His loss of balance sent him dangerously toward the edge.

"Careful there, pal," the voice said. Just Middle Manager felt a hand grab his arm and pull him safely away from jeopardy. "You might want to back away from there. There is no reason for you, or me either, for that matter, to go over that cliff," the voice spoke as the arm rescued him.

"That was a little scary," the voice went on to say, as Just Middle Manager gained his balance, stepping clear of the hazard. "One should be careful getting too close to such danger," the voice added.

Just Middle Manger wasn't sure what to say. The person standing in front of him had, thankfully, rescued him from extreme danger. But, at the same time, it was the speaking of this stranger coming from behind Just Middle Manager that had actually put him into peril to begin with. Rather than say the wrong thing, Just Middle Manager didn't say anything directly, but looked back toward the danger and said, "That was close, entirely too close for my comfort."

> Insight: The appetite of a leader following the style of Leader Orphan is always to be careful and to see that danger may lurk around any and all corners. "Street-smart" Orphan sees vulnerability in life, having the ability to see possible dangers preying ahead with open eyes. The Orphan views everyone as being equal to each other, so leadership is more shared than it might be in a forced hierarchal structure. Leader Orphan will inspire and desire those they lead to be vigilant and watchful, rewarding those who spot possible danger first. At the end of the day the Orphan might say it was a great day because he or she survived it, rescuing self and others from the edge of destruction or certain peril.

"Well, thankfully you now have some temporary refuge. Of course, stepping away from the edge of the cliff may only be a momentary respite. For if you judge that you can actually navigate your way through this hazard simply based upon your discourse with Leader Innocent, then go ahead and return to the earth's edge. But I shall not venture to rescue you a second time."

"My name is Leader Orphan, by the way. Glad to meet up with you," Leader Orphan said, stepping closer to Just Middle Manager. Once again, Orphan extended a hand, but this time it was in a formal position of greeting rather than an offer to pull someone out of danger. Just Middle Manager shook the presented hand, albeit awkwardly.

Having released hands, they both leaned carefully over the edge of the ravine to survey where Just Middle Manager might have fallen to his harm. Again, Just Middle Manger shook his head in relief and then stepped clearly away from the earth's rim. He stared briefly at his rescuer. Leader Orphan had introduced himself, and they had both shook hands; but Just Middle Manager wasn't sure if he was ready to trust this savior. That thought must have revealed itself in his facial expression.

"I relish that expression on your face," Orphan said with the appearance of a smile adding to the statement. Actually, Orphan's smile was closer to a malevolent smirk. Leader Orphan's life had savored a look of skepticism for both Orphan and for others. The facial expression that Just Middle Manager was now presenting was the look Leader Orphan thought all should convey to the world around them.

"What look might that be?" Just Middle Manager asked, still sizing up the person before him. Only slightly taller than Just Middle Manager, Leader Orphan looked like any ordinary person one might meet on any of life's many journeys. Orphan didn't have any physical characteristics that caused Just Middle Manager to be alarmed or any characteristics that would be cause for one to notice Orphan. For that matter, this was what actually caused Just Middle Manager to pause and guard his trust; Leader Orphan looked entirely like anyone and everyone. He looked like *every person,* not someone to mistrust, but not someone you openly trusted, either.

"'What look,' you ask? That look of skepticism you now portray on your face," Leader Orphan answered, having retreated farther away from the cliff. Orphan had actually stepped slightly off the path, taking refuge near the mouth of a very dark and dreary looking cave. Like Orphan, the cave appeared as though it was both pleasing and perilous, simultaneously.

Insight: The Orphan style is a leveling approach to life: We are all the same, and there is little that allows others to be something better or mightier than others. This approach to life motivates Orphan to take on a benign look, having no desire to distinguish him or herself from others in a particular group.

Upon seeing the cave, Just Middle Manager thought he must

have passed it on his journey but had evidently missed it entirely. He was suddenly caught in the thought that if he had had his eyes more open to the path before him, he might have seen both the cave and the cliff that obviously surprised him. But he was too enraptured with the light and heat of the sun to see these dangers or possibly others. The beauty of the day had hidden the dangers of the path. *What else could I have missed,* he thought?

Just Middle Manager consulted the map he still held firmly in his hand to see if it showed this, or any, shadowy place of retreat. While he looked at the diagram, a questioning look on his face must have conveyed even more skepticism; Leader Orphan appeared actually entertained with Just Middle Manager's cynical looks.

"That look on your face ..." Orphan began again, seeing Just Middle Manager was apparently not going to engage in much verbal jabbing, "is a look of not just skepticisms but of true doubt. And I perceive that it might possibly be directed toward me. Is there a reason why you have lost the look of optimism you had when you passed by my home a few moments ago? It was that look of hope you were equipped with and given by Leader Innocent," Leader Orphan asked and further explained, ending the question and comments with a long sigh.

"I do not mean to disparage you, personally, my friend," Just Middle Manager said, directly responding to Leader Orphan for the first time. "It is just that I was so caught up in the thought of the blessings of where I was going and the brightness of the day that I totally missed both the danger of the cliff and any possible haven you may have offered. Please forgive me."

"No reason to ask forgiveness my good fellow. We are both but travelers on the same highway of life and have—I am sure—succumbed to the same gaffes as well," Leader Orphan responded. In the answer there was actually a sense of concern and empathy replacing the tone of sarcasm to which Just Middle Manager had already grown accustomed.

"Thanks for understanding," Just Middle Manager said, also

noticing a change in Orphan's demeanor and facial expressions. The warmth of Orphan's response suddenly caused Just Middle Manager to have a small, but affectionate sentiment for Orphan and for this emerging life philosophy. That change in his own attitude caused Just Middle Manager to think a little clearer about the concept of skepticism and scrutiny surrounding the issues in life, especially leadership. *Perhaps,* he thought to himself, *the skepticism he is now utilizing might have been useful in his earlier walk up the path.*

Feeling a little more comfortable with his own thought process, he felt as though he should take another look at his map. Suddenly, in clear view on the map before him, he noticed the markings. The cliff and the cave were not only visible on the map he held, but, as Just Middle Manager could now plainly see, they were remarkably obvious. *How could I have missed this before?* he asked himself.

"I don't understand how I didn't see this on the map," Just Middle Manager stated, talking to the chart more than to Leader Orphan.

"I would be delighted to enlighten you concerning your missteps," Orphan offered, not concerned whether it would offend Just Middle Manager while at the same time being careful to not create too much vulnerability with the statement. (Orphan, though appearing to change demeanor for a moment, once again continued with a vigilance of skepticism. It was, after all, a born nature.)

"Please enlighten me," Just Middle Manager said, looking up from the map and giving Orphan his full consideration. He was eager to learn, and since his heart was still racing from his earlier fright, he was even more interested in not repeating his prior error of judgment.

In being so eager, Leader Orphan could see that Just Middle Manager had once again dropped his guard and replaced his newfound skepticism with Innocent's optimism. So, with a sigh, Orphan began his revelation. "It was easy to see that this would come upon you. I knew it the minute you left Leader Innocent up the path. You were so entranced with the flowery words of Innocent that you forgot to use the very gifts of life you were provided at a young age. All of us were born with a sense of innocence, but as we mature, we should also be equipped with a sense for danger. You, in your spellbound optimistic state *and* focus on the hope of a bright new day, were blinded to the very skills you were so gifted in life. Leader Innocent does this to those who drink from his pool of hope. But, alas, they eventually wind up at that cliff and standing outside my place of refuge. Not all survive, unfortunately. Some do; some don't." These words were accompanied by a small retreat closer to the mouth of the cave. Orphan climbed up onto a perch constructed out of wooden boxes. The makeshift pulpit was imprinted with the words, "broken dreams and failed expectations."

"You see," Orphan added, pointing with his arm extended toward the path Just Middle Manager had just traveled. "I could see you coming just as you left Leader Innocent up that passageway."

"But I found his words so helpful in my journey to Celestial City of Influence and the lightening of this load on my back," Just Middle Manager responded. He did not want to anger or offend Leader Orphan, but at the same time, he did want to hold to the hope that he had discovered when he was with Leader Innocent. What he received from Innocent was a great feeling of hope and possibility offering bright illumination to him. Just Middle Manager didn't want to return to the dark place of despair from which he had come. That was another cliff in life he wanted to avoid.

"Words do not get you to and through the large valley in front of you," Orphan continued. "Your destination is, indeed, rich with affluence. But the blessings afforded in Celestial City of Influence are undiscovered by simple words of hope and happiness. You must ever be vigilant, if you wish to arrive both unharmed and still equipped." In this response, Orphan did not worry about tact, rather seeking clarity over harmony. Orphan's concern was for Just Middle Manager's understanding, not his approval.

"Equipped?" Just Middle Manager asked, his ears perking at Orphan's use of the word.

"Yes, equipped to be the Next Great Leader. That is why you are traveling to Celestial City of Influence with such a load on your back, isn't it? Aren't you looking for answers to the many questions you carry so that you might be renamed Next Great Leader?"

> Insight: When faced with problems, Leader Orphan is on constant vigilance to prevent being blindsided, rather being prepared. Because the Orphan life is a "leveling" life that sees others as the Orphan may see themselves, the solution for one may be the solution for all. In the face of difficulty the Orphan may become fatalistic and even cynical. Orphans might not trust everyone, as they are always alert for potential problems on the horizon. Therefore they may ignore others' solutions, choosing their own believed way of safety first.

"Why, yes, but how did you know such a thing?" Just Middle Manager asked, remembering that when he encountered Leader Innocent, it was needful to explain the pack on his back. But Leader Orphan apparently didn't need such an explanation.

"I have seen so many travelers pass by with similar aspirations. It is my nature to look ahead, to be aware, and to possess constant attentiveness for what may or may not happen. I sense that you, like all others who travel this path, have drunk full from that same spoiled pool of Innocent and simply lost your bearings. You and I may be the same in regard to generating life miscalculations, but whereas I have found solace in this cave for protection, you are still gazing at the light, having lost your focus on the map before you."

Leader Orphan, as always, was enjoying the matriculation of Just Middle Manager. Orphan rejoiced at being able to better prepare Just Middle Manager for his journey to Celestial City of Influence and to sway him away from his unguided allegiance toward the words of Leader Innocent. Orphan so enjoyed this and was so familiar with the conversation they were having; the question Just Middle Manager was about to pose was not a surprise. Orphan had been down this path many times and knew what was coming before Just Middle Manager even knew he was to solicit it. Orphan was seldom blindsided.

"But don't you see some reliability in Leader Innocent's words?" Just Middle Manager asked, his burden once again feeling awkward and heavy. Even in the way he asked the question he could tell he wasn't sure he wanted to or could ever trust Leader Innocent again. He quickly gazed over his shoulder toward the cliff that came close to ending his journey. Having thought about that moment, he took another step toward Leader Orphan's sanctuary. Dark as the cave appeared, that one step seemed to put him closer to safety than the danger he once faced.

"Innocent's words are his words. I dare not deny them, nor will I validate them. I only offer my language with the hope you will be vigilant in your walk and wary in your progress," Leader Orphan said, sounding more humble than he actually was.

"So it is your *hope* that I will take to heart your counsels and deny those from Leader Innocent?" Just Middle Manager asked. "You would have me place my hope in *your* words rather than the hope offered by Innocent, would you not?"

"I would have you place your hope in that which will lighten your load," Leader Orphan answered. Orphan wanted to avoid the debate between the two leaders, for it often found its way into the conversations with so many travelers.

"If it lightens your load to walk headlong over the cliff, who am I to draw such a judgment?" Orphan continued. "But if you will consult your map and heed my words, you might find not only your place in the journey but answers to the many questions you carry, as well."

As he considered Leader Orphan's words, Just Middle Manager leaned against the entrance of the cave and pondered both his place on the map and the words of Orphan. It was true; while looking heavenly for hope without considering the urgent path in front of him, he had met with certain jeopardy. *Perhaps not now, but eventually,* he thought. However, prior to his dialogue with Leader Innocent, he was so engulfed with the dangers and dilemma of the present path that he had little energy to move forward in his undertaking. It was during this thought the epiphany came to him. The notion came to him with such vigor and volume that Just Middle Manager screamed with glee. As a result, Leader Orphan almost fell off his unstable perch.

"I shall take you both as part of my leadership style. The one shall balance the other," Just Middle Manager shouted. He was so happy with himself that he barely noticed Leader Orphan's loss of balance. (He didn't notice either that the load on his back had diminished in size and weight.)

Reaching out to steady Leader Orphan, Just Middle Manager joked, "There, we're even." A small smile came over Just Middle Manager. Not a smile that conveyed any trust but rather like a glance one traveler would give to another having found them in a similar state one time or another.

Leader Orphan got off the box perch and was glad for the established connection with Just Middle Manager. Orphan never wanted to be considered as a bookend in regard to Innocent, but the term had been used before in dialogues of the past. Not every traveler on the path to Celestial City of Influence had drawn such a conclusion as Just Middle Manager, but Leader Orphan knew that those that did balance Innocent and Orphan would have more success at being named Next Great Leader.

"With this fine discovery made, you may want to once again consider the map you hold firmly in hand," Leader Orphan suggested.

Just Middle Manager looked, once again, down to his map. There, as bright and bold as the noon day sun, he saw the path he must take. The path marked on the map, surprisingly, that best offered escape from the cliff and the furtherance of his journey, went directly into the Leader Orphan's cave. Like the doorway to a dark, winding stairway, the cave was but the beginning to another path. This new way would begin in darkness but would, eventually, come out directly behind the refreshment of a waterfall on the valley floor. In order to reach the fruit in the basin before him, Just Middle Manager discovered he simply had to hold on to his hope for the many treasures of Celestial City of Influence while at the same time being vigilant as he descended the dark steps that lay before him.

"How did I miss this before," Just Middle Manager asked.

Leader Orphan didn't want to say but forced the following. "Perhaps your latest epiphany not only lightened your load but opened your leadership vision as well?"

It was only then that Just Middle Manager even noticed his burden was lighter. With that realization, another smile came across his face, and he turned to head down the tunnel, only briefly acknowledging Leader Orphan. Unlike his departure from Leader Innocent, Just Middle Manager believed he was not only heading toward Celestial City of Influence, he was gaining ground on answering the question that lay heavy in his backpack.

The progress Just Middle Manager was making didn't really help Roy in his quest for sleep, regretfully. Still unable to settle himself, Roy rolled over onto his opposite side, simultaneously giving Jill a hug in his sleep. He wouldn't remember that he did so, as he fell even deeper into a sleepy state. Jill was not asleep. Something was still keeping her awake; it might have been the chocolate chip cookies she had found in the night stand drawer and had finished off while Roy was tossing and turning.

As Just Middle Manager was descending the steps down from the cave, Leader Orphan shouted one last word of warning into the cave's darkness, "Make sure you stay well alert for Ego and Envy. They are desperate twins who only wish harm to the Next Great Leader."

Orphan's warning would have been a great message for any weary traveler headed for Celestial City of Influence. But in his haste, Just Middle Manager was already standing at the bottom of the rock staircase. He was standing directly behind a wall of water coming from above the valley floor and pouring over the worn rocks below. All he could hear was the thunder of the water as it hit the stone basin. He didn't hear the warning about Ego and Envy.

He did vaguely see something through the partition of water. The mist and the natural splatter of the water made most things in the valley either totally void or partially unrecognizable. But, in the distance, Just Middle Manager could make out what looked like a warrior. *What is a warrior doing in this beautiful valley,* he thought.

	Insight Tips for putting *Leader Orphan* to work in your own Leadership Style - *Successfully*
1	Keep your eyes open. Don't get so caught up in your ideas that you lose sight of the dangers those same ideas (or, perhaps those of others) may present. Vigilance is a blessing and a curse. Embrace both its beauty and its burden.
2	Remember that although we all may be similar, we are not all the same. Because the Orphan has a tendency to be a leveling philosophy, make sure you allow others to aspire to be something greater than they may want to be or greater than you may want to be. Leveling for the sake of leveling is not a positive attribute. Think of the parents who want the child to walk in their footsteps. Sometimes children have to get their own wings for life. True, ducks don't give birth to eagles, but some ducks fly while others only quack.
3	Working with others to accomplish a common goal is one of your strengths. But working with others demands a certain level of trust. Even though others may have hurt you in the past, be willing to trust again. It is a worthy character quality to possess even if it didn't help in some other story or some other life moment.
4	Don't resolve to live at a certain place in a certain time or with a certain experience. Set your sights higher sometimes. It is okay to seek safety, but only if you are actually safe. You may be simply endangering yourself further by placing yourself in a predictable position of mediocrity. Being comfortable isn't necessarily being safe.
5	Life is full of difficulties. If you live (or maybe more accurately, *don't live*) your life controlled by them, you will not only miss out on both the great blessings life can bring you, but you will also bring others down with you. Face the difficulties with a plan to live above them, or with them, if they can't be defeated. However, don't let the difficulties of life defeat *you*; manipulate them so they can define your character and style.

Words of Discipline and Determination from Leader Warrior

Just Middle Manager couldn't believe his eyes. He had never been in a valley so full of bounty. It was as though the spoils of many wars had been deposited onto one basin floor. With the richness of the sight before him, he felt he must be getting closer to Celestial City of Influence. The very sight of the many treasures dancing before his eyes loosened the load on his back. *Truly this is what "Influence" looks like,* he thought.

Although the blessings he beheld were beautiful and appeared ripe for the picking, Just Middle Manager had one dilemma: A barrier stood between him and this glorious prize. Positioned before him was a large figure that looked half warrior and half competitive athlete. Tall, strong, sleek, and trim, the figure was positioned as if on guard before the treasures. The figure's feet were prepared for swift running, and the large muscles of the arms glistened in the valley sun. The medals of many battles won hung across the chest, a personal Wall of Fame. From a distance the figure was overwhelming, but as Just Middle Manager approached, it seemed even more daunting.

"Hello, friend," Just Middle Manager called, approaching hesitantly. As he drew closer, he slowed his gate slowly, noticing that the figure had grown more alert with each approaching step he took.

After losing his way on the prior path and nearly walking off a cliff, Just Middle Manager thought that this would be a good time for him to practice the instructions he had recently learned from Orphan. (He only now recalled hearing Orphan warn him to *beware* of something. Was this figure the focus of Orphan's warning?)

"Hold fast, traveler," the figure shouted. "Declare your intent or beware of my own," the voice warned.

Just Middle Manager stopped his forward movement as a swift steed would halt at the edge of an exposed overhang. In hindsight he would come to realize that stopping was a good thing. But, the fear he was showing on his face was not. The figure before him seized onto Just Middle Manager's fright. Like a wild dog smelling the scent of its next victim, the image before him gathered more energy and excitement. Just Middle Manager was only able to gather more terror and trepidation.

"Traveler, if you wish to travel through this valley, your fear will have to be sheathed and your courage drawn," the figure stated, while at the same time seeming to relax into an "at rest" position.

"Do you travel alone or do you lead a band? Are you an ally or an antagonist?" Each question shot out as a dart towards Just Middle Manager's small frame.

"Do you intend to engage with me in combat or to simply pass through Victory Valley in this fearful state? Is that backpack your courage or your failed weapons of warfare? My name is Warrior, and if you are a friend and in need of assistance, I tender my hand. But if you are a rival, I extend to you the armaments of battle."

As the Warrior spoke, each of the questions landed onto Just Middle Manager's pack. Once again it began to shift, with awkwardness replacing the self-control he had established after his meetings with leaders

Insight: The appetite of a leader following the style of Leader Warrior is about winning and about securing the victory, no matter the opposition. Warrior sees life as something to be conquered and uses determination and pride as guiding values to secure the victory. The Warrior may view others as either those needing rescue, or competition for a would-be prize. Leader Warrior will inspire and desire those they lead to be competitive and battle sound, rewarding those who fight harder and longer first. At the end of the day the Warrior might say it was a great day because he or she won, was victorious in battle, and secured the reward.

Innocent and Orphan. "Your questions land upon me as unneeded weight and as burdens that I am not willing or able to bear," Just Middle Manager began his response. "Perhaps your intent is well measured, but your manner is found wanting." Just Middle Manager continued speaking with a sudden sense of valor, surprising both Warrior and himself.

Warrior appeared pleased with the response of Just Middle Manager, but not because he showed valor. Warrior's disposition was converted by the fact that he now saw a willing adversary rather than a fearful soul, lost and alone on a road of combat.

"So, you have found your voice. But, have you found your skill?" Warrior took a step forward, drawing the largest of the weapons that hung about his waist. "I have been hoping for a tussle or two for the day. The valley has been very calm since the last weary traveler was dispatched—quite quickly I might add." Warrior seemed to be taking great solace in recounting even a brief memory of a past battle. He seemed to be transported back in time, reveling in a marvelous memory of conquest.

"Good friend, stop!" Just Middle Manager quickly shouted. He took a step back and to the left, finding a small rock formation that might offer a small refuge should Warrior commensurate the drawn sword with an actual attack. "Why are you so bent on combat today or on any day for that matter? I am Just Middle Manager, a weary traveler on the road to Celestial City of Influence, hoping upon arrival to be worthy enough to become Next Great Leader. I have no desire to engage in conflict with you or for you. I am but a seeker of truth and a traveler of hope. I only wish to battle the weight of the pack on my back and to discover my own leadership plight, thus relieving this unwanted load."

Warrior paused for a moment, appearing to collect many thoughts (or, as Just Middle Manager mused, deciding what part of his body Warrior would apply the sword he held so intently).

The sword in Warrior's hand began to lower, slowly, eventually finding its return home along Warrior's side. Taking a step closer toward Just Middle Manager, Warrior extended the right hand.

Although leery and still remembering Orphan's words to be aware of vulnerability, Just Middle Manager offered his hand in return. What followed next caused Just Middle Manager to both accelerate in anxiety and suddenly feel at great peace. Warrior's hand not only took Just Middle Manager's hand but slid up his forearm as well. Interlocking hands to forearms as some medieval knight, Warrior pulled Just Middle Manager toward the medals that hung off the chest and embraced him. As two athletes caught in an uncomfortably long chest bump, Warrior and Just Middle Manager were united.

"If you are a troubled traveler, I offer you both my skill and my determination," Warrior stated, releasing Just Middle Manager back to the ground (although during the embrace, Just Middle Manager didn't even realize he had been lifted off the ground). "I am a skilled leader and can assist you with the problem you now face or any you might face in the future. We shall chart the course of your travel to make preparations for the road that lies ahead and to alleviate that cumbersome burden you carry," Warrior spoke, head nodding to the pack on Just Middle Manager's back.

As Warrior finished the brief discourse, the chiseled arms of strength whirled Just Middle Manager around and began to take the pack off his back. Although Just Middle Manager was anxious to find respite from the weight, he wasn't totally sure he wanted Warrior, or anyone for that matter, removing the pack without asking permission first. Warrior noticed neither the

Insight: When faced with problems, the appetite of Leader Warrior is to begin looking for solutions and strategies. Warrior switches quickly from combatant warrior to engaged hero. Drawing upon skills obtained in past battles and rescue operations to solve current dilemmas, Warrior may begin salvage formulas, even when those suffering have neither asked nor wanted liberation. When those formulas fail, however, Warrior may simply work harder and longer at the same strategies hoping for different results. Although setting aside the combat mode, Warrior will strive to solve the problem with the same determination of warfare, viewing the problem, or those who caused it, as the new enemy and/or rival.

apprehension nor the uneasiness in Just Middle Manager's demeanor. Warrior was on a new mission, not one of combat but of support. Just Middle Manager was no longer a rival fit for battle but a sufferer needing salvation.

"Thank you for lowering my pack," Just Middle Manager stated falsely as Warrior lowered the pack on the ground. He would have preferred to remove it himself, but he was glad it was off his shoulders, even if done so without proper protocol.

Together, they both took relief upon the rock formation previously perceived as a refuge from danger. It was only until they both sat upon the small structure that Just Middle Manager could see that the rocks never would have protected him from Warrior if an attack had ensued.

Ignoring his thanks, having picked up on the disingenuous nature of it, Warrior nevertheless began a strategy for solving Just Middle Manager's quandary. "The weight of this pack is not really that heavy at all. But I shall still give you what support, encouragement, and direction I can. I have assisted many travelers in similar difficulties and find it a source of energy to once again use my skills this time for your service. Regretfully, I do think your cause for alarm is a might overstated. Perhaps the struggle you have is not the weight of the pack but the weakness of your back."

Just Middle Manager stood quickly, insulted by Warrior's statement and the insinuation that he was not able to carry the load he had already tracked across many miles, up and down numerous winding paths. His quick stance not only startled Warrior, who had become at ease on the rocks, but also gave cause for the sheathed sword to be returned to a ready position. Standing toe-to-toe, both Warrior and Just Middle Manager appeared as combatants on the valley floor; only one was armed.

Insight: Warriors Leaders might often see problems based upon the weaknesses of those they are trying to rescue. Pointing out those weaknesses may be viewed as a necessary strategy during the rescuing process. **NOTE**: Warrior might return to combat mode quickly when perceived to be provoked or threatened, even if the provocation or threat is not real but only imagined.

"Please," Just Middle Manager shouted, "I have no desire to compete with you. I was just taken aback by your articulation and view of my state." Just Middle Manager was careful how he uttered his words. He knew he was not only out-armed but truly was no warrior himself.

Sheathing the sword a second time, Warrior once again took a post on the rock formation. Warrior looked at Just Middle Manager with a brazen face and said, "I can see why you are having difficulty on your journey, my friend. Your inability to respond properly to criticism is a weakness travelers on the way to Celestial City of Influence can ill afford."

"Criticism I can grasp. It is your constant combative nature that I find not only repulsive but ..." Just Middle Manager paused, looking for just the right word to complete his sentence as well as his complaint concerning Warrior's tact.

"Combative?" Warrior spoke up, not giving Just Middle Manager time to find the word he was looking for.

"Yes, combative!"

"Some may view my approach combative, so you are not alone in your assessment," Warrior replied, drinking in the criticism offered by Just Middle Manager. (Warrior didn't want to be guilty of refusing criticism.) "But," Warrior continued, not really believing Just Middle Manager's analysis was at all accurate, "Those seeking the true meaning of leadership find my approach much more favorable than most styles. Perhaps you would do well to adopt it as your own as you travel your journey? It would serve you well all the way to *Celestial*."

"What portion of your nature, exactly, would you have me mirror? Would it be the combative side or the area lacking diplomacy and charm?"

Warrior chuckled slightly and then, with little emotion, replied, "Both!"

"Both? You do have a big ego, don't you?"

Upon hearing the word *ego*, Warrior stood as if "attention" had been called by a senior officer. Once again, Warrior placed a hand on the sword hanging from the belt of armor. Looking first left and right, Warrior asked, "Are you aware of Ego? Have you seen him? What about his evil companion Envy? Have you spotted him as well? Are they lurking in the shadows?"

"What are you talking about," Just Middle Manager asked (still not recalling Orphan's earlier warning).

"You accused me of being egotistical, and that can only come from he who lurks in the shadow and attempts to sway every leader: Ego, himself."

"I know nothing of this one, Ego, or of the other, Envy. But, I do believe you are so bent on combat and conflict that I would not want to be in the company of either."

"And you would do well, my friend, to keep that state of mind," Warrior said, placing one foot on the rocks rather than resuming a seated position. Warrior's eyes scanned the horizon like a hawk, looking for any threat, real or imagined.

"I simply believe," Just Middle Manager went on, hoping to return the conversation to his previous point, "that you are much too confrontational for me to mimic, and you seem to not care that you are."

"Perhaps my ways do not meet with your approval," Warrior stated, returning to their combative discourse, "but more importantly, the effectiveness of my leadership may not be measured in the same paradigm to which you are accustomed. Perhaps it is not my caustic nature that offends you, but that you are limited by your own range of knowledge. You may not be able to view my strengths as meaningful and needed because your view is obstructed by your current distorted model of leadership. I believe most successful leaders view life through my clear lens: Problems are to be solved in a winning manner, and people are to be lead and challenged, or rescued, if needed. All this wealth on the valley floor was accumulated by aggressive leadership and a winning mentality. You can't lead when you think you might lose. Others will not follow a losing mentality. People like to know they are on the winning side. Winners are promoted. Losers are ... well, losers."

Just Middle Manager sat for a moment. He needed to think through what Warrior was actually saying. Although caustic as an approach, Warrior might have a point to offer. The pack of questions that currently sat at his feet mandated that he pursue the premise offered by Warrior.

There was time to muse over these thoughts, anyway. Warrior indicated he heard a sound in some bushes a few yards away and was off to fight another war with a possible opponent. As Just Middle Manager watched, he was somewhat amused by Warrior's tenacity, although he was put out by Warrior's constant need to be right. Warrior seemed to view the world and situations in an *either/or* mindset, black or white. Just Middle Manager had thought life was more complicated and preferred the *both/and* approach, many hues of gray.

Warrior's arguments were compelling and convincing. Perhaps the way to lead others was to make sure you had a winning attitude and were willing to fight for that in which you believe. You may be wrong at times, but the need to fight through life's tribulations and lead others with a mentality that you *may be* right or that you are eager to *get to right* at all costs is a strong contention.

Just Middle Manager was naturally passive. Watching Warrior, sword in hand, poking and prodding a clump of bushes to make sure there was nothing dangerous lurking inspired Just Middle Manager. Somehow he didn't think there was a threat out there, but just knowing Warrior was making sure that there wasn't gave him a sense of peace and a feeling of tranquility in his soul. What Innocent offered in hope and Orphan presented concerning vulnerability, Warrior portrayed in an attitude of preparation.

Yes, Warrior was bold and confrontational, but there was some assurance in that style that gave Just Middle Manager a sense of courage by which to augment his hope.

"Sorry for running off like that," Warrior said, approaching from Just Middle Manager's opposite flank. "One cannot be too careful out there. But vigilance has to be acted upon, or it is simply fear in a bolted closet."

"Yes, I am beginning to see your point," Just Middle Manager answered, wondering how Warrior had gone from one flank to the other without his knowing or seeing it done. "I see that your courage mixed with skill and determination would be pleasant additions to my own desire to become Next Great Leader. But, is there anything you fear?"

"No!" Warrior responded quickly and assuredly.

"Don't all men fear something?"

"Fear is for the faint hearted. It is for followers to not only possess but to put on display each day," Warrior snapped. "And believe me, if you ever lead anyone, they will more than tell you their fears. The only thing I fear is the fear of not being able to handle fear, of not having the power to overcome a fear I face."

Insight: Since an archetype has both a shiny side and a shadowy side, most don't see their shadowy side, preferring rather to view themselves on the shiny side only. Knowing both the shiny and the shadowy sides, however, enables the archetype to work more productively and confidently. Discover the shiny side and use it. Be aware of the shadowy side and seek to avoid its pitfalls!

"*Impotency* would be harmful to a warrior of your caliber or for any warrior for that matter," Just Middle Manager said, not really knowing why he used such a word or if he should.

"Impotency? I can assure you that I am not impotent!" Warrior shouted, looking around carefully again from left to right, this time not looking for a possible rival but anyone who may have heard the use of such a word in the context of and same sentence as "Warrior."

"I only meant that not having power would be a trait unbefitting Warrior," Just Middle Manager stated quickly, fearing Warrior might at any time return to the belt of armor.

"Loss of power would manifest itself how?" Warrior asked for the first time during their conversation, seeking information rather than imparting it. Not surprisingly, even when asking the question, Warrior was careful the tone used would not display a weakness or a possible defect in character.

"I don't know," Just Middle Manager offered hesitantly. "Perhaps it would be when the power becomes a liability."

"How could power be a liability?" Warrior asked, starting to take on even more of a posture of learning rather than teaching.

"My journey is about that very question," Just Middle Manager stated. "I desire to discover the best style of leadership for myself and to be faithful to it. Considering that a leader's strength could also be a weakness assists me in that quest. Your insights and questions have given me much to ponder."

Warrior paused, not really knowing if the insights Just Middle Manager had gleaned were something provided through skill or stumbled upon as though walking along a path only to discover some rare delicacy growing directly on the trail in front of you.

"Perhaps my use of power is better served if I am aware of those weaknesses myself," Warrior stated. "If a desire to be right and to win is my strength, then the desire to always be right and to always win may be my Achilles' heal. And we know what a weakness did to warrior Achilles!"

Just Middle Manager almost chuckled that Warrior was comparing the two of them. *But why not,* he thought. *Warriors are warriors, and along with their strengths, there are apparent weaknesses. Good warriors are aware of both. The fallen warrior may be the one who only thought in terms of personal vigor and not of practical limitations.*

"Perhaps on your journey, you may be able to use the lessons learned here in Victory Valley, and I will be able to use them in my quest to be triumphant in future battles. Being disciplined and determined in one's virtues will make one victorious and superior," Warrior added.

"I will certainly be able to use them, Warrior. I see that wanting to win, standing for what I believe in, and fighting for it is a worthy honor to hold. I also see that rescuing others is something I shall pride myself on—"

"But, only if they want the help," Warrior chimed in, finishing the sentence for him with a small smile appearing across the once brash face. "May I help you with your pack?" Warrior asked, noticing Just Middle Manager was lifting his backpack to return it to its carry position.

"Yes, you may help," Just Middle Manager responded. As the load was being placed back into location, he couldn't help but notice the load was not only less awkward but also lighter and less burdensome as well. Perhaps, it was Warrior's firm hand assisting. *Or, was it the gained knowledge Warrior allowed me to see? Time will tell which of the two are most true,* he thought.

"Continue your quest with this new courage for right and with vigor to fight," Warrior stated. "You must head further down the road toward Celestial City of Influence, but beware of Ego *and* Envy, for, as I said, they lurk in the darkness."

"I wish I had time to discuss more with you about your warrior ways and of Ego and Envy, but I must make haste as darkness is setting, and I would prefer to be out of the open valley before nightfall," Just Middle Manager said as he began to look down the path that still lay before him. "I fear I have many battles to fight before I reach my journey's end and can ill afford to stop for any length of time. I am sure there is more we could teach each other, but the small lessons you have taught me have already lessened the large load I carry. I look forward to a future duel of wit and wisdom."

"Take care, my friend. You are already beginning to think and talk like a warrior. I am glad I was able to provide some assistance and rescue you from your small quandary," Warrior said, once again viewing Just Middle Manager as someone to rescue rather than a co-warrior on the same road of life.

Warrior will always be Warrior, Just Middle Manager thought. But that type of strength was something he thought he should also possess.

As he picked up his pace down the beaten path, he gathered more and more courage. His resolve was to mirror the shiny side of Leader Warrior (the discipline, the desire to fight for beliefs, and the development of both a winning attitude and a winning strategy for life), while at the same time avoiding the shadowy sides of Warrior (having to always be right, jumping in to rescue when others may not need or desire the help, and not allowing the desire for power and closure over problems to cloud his view of the many possible options that are always available).

As Just Middle Manager walked farther down the path, he turned to take one last look at Warrior. Since he was so far down the path, he could only make out Warrior poking around more bushes with a drawn sword. Regretfully, as he took a few more steps and one final look at Warrior, he failed to see the danger that lay directly in the path before him. Head over heels he fell, rolling and rolling down a decline so sharp that it was impossible for him to stop his momentum. Like a snowball gaining size, he felt himself gathering sticks, twigs, and grass as he tumbled. When he came to a halt he had collected debris in almost every crevice of his body. He wasn't sure what had happened, but he knew he was in a bad spot since he couldn't move. The weight on his back was pinning him firmly against a large log. He knew he was too far from Warrior for his voice to be heard, but nevertheless, he yelled with all his might, "Help! Help! Someone help me!"

Insight Tips for putting *Leader Warrior* to work in your own Leadership Style - *Successfully*	
1	Don't always be *argumentative.* The Warrior tendency is to want to fight over things believed or held to. However, wars always have causalities. You may be right and have a correct strategy to win the fight, but you may lose the war or a friend in the process. Learn how to employ your desire to win the argument, debate or battle in more collaborative ways.
2	Know the shadowy side of your nature is to be *competitive.* Everything doesn't have to be a contest to win. Failure to see the shadow may prevent others from viewing the shiny side (your desire for excellence and for winning) in a positive manner. You don't have to lose, but you have to avoid always having to compete.
3	Don't always feel as though you have to rescue those in trouble. They may need rescuing, but you may not be the person for the job. That doesn't mean your skills are lacking, but that others may not view a rescue as the answer to their problem. Others sometimes want to and need to solve their problems themselves. However, if you do attempt a rescue and it doesn't work, it may not be your skills that are lacking. The old adage *you can bring a horse to water but you can't make him drink* may be in play in your rescue operation.
4	Don't view all problems through the lens of someone's failures or deficiency. Sometimes even the strongest of warriors run into problems. Everyone has failures and defects. Learn to have a healthy view of those around you and of yourself as well. Admitting your lack of skill or that you need to learn something isn't the end of the world. It may very well be the beginning of new growth and great influence and power.
5	Don't view power and strength as the end but rather virtues to use along the path of life. Life should not be defined by how much power you have or how much strength you can accumulate. Use your power and strength to serve others. Doing so will provide you with even more power and strength. True strength and power is when you know how to use the two in your service of others.

Words of Service and Help from Leader Caregiver

Just Middle Manager knew his cry for help would not reach Warrior's ears. (He didn't know that Warrior's ears had already been sequestered by another traveler perceived by Warrior to also be in trouble. The victim didn't know he was in turmoil, but nevertheless, Warrior was on the way to rescue him.) Just Middle Manager, obviously in great need, lay struggling on the ground alone, or that is what he thought.

"You are in great need of help, good sir. Those provisions in your pack have become a real sense of struggle for you. Let me assist you." Just Middle Manager couldn't see who was talking, but the tone was not that of Warrior. Warrior's coarseness had been replaced by a sound of care and compassion.

From above his prone position, he could see the silhouette of someone who was not only coming to his aide but who was also blocking the heat of the setting sun. The shadow was not large, and somehow, through the character conveyed by the voice, Just Middle Manager was not afraid. He felt two hands gently move the pack of weight that had rolled on top of his outstretched left arm. The hands were gentle, and although Just Middle Manager knew intellectually you couldn't tell through a sense of touch, the hands felt kind, in complete harmony with the voice speaking.

As the person moved slightly to one side, the evening glare of the sun struck Just Middle Manager once again, momentarily obstructing his vision. He could not make out the face of the person standing over him, but he could see from the palms of the hands now releasing the pack from his back that it was someone who was not afraid of hard work. Each palm bore the callous tattoos of what must be meticulous and difficult work. Yet the rough appearance of each was completely overpowered by the warmth of benevolence.

"Let me slowly move this pack to the left, if that is alright?" the voice continued, asking but moving ahead without waiting for a response from Just Middle Manager. Slowly and carefully, the pack was slid aside, and Just Middle Manager was able to find relief from the log that was pressing against the right side of his body.

"Are you feeling better? Are you okay? Do you feel anything broken?" Each question was coming from the figure that stood just off center from Just Middle Manager, allowing the sun to once again cause his eyes to squint.

"I'm sorry, how rude. You are not in the best situation to answer any questions. And I haven't even introduced myself. My name is Caregiver," the statements coming as the figure moved back in the line of the sun to cast a shadow once again across Just Middle Manager's face. "I am very glad to meet you, although certainly not under these circumstances."

Giving Just Middle Manager a hand, Caregiver lifted him to his feet.

"I saw your tumble from above," Caregiver said, escorting him away from the log to find

Insight: The appetite of a leader following the style of Leader Caregiver is about helping and serving others. Caregiver sees life as consisting of a series of events where people are helped and assisted with their problems. The Caregiver may view others typically as in some variety of trouble or conflict. The Caregiver's own need to assist others may motivate them to look for injury or pain in others (real or imagined) that they can personally alleviate by an act of kindness (even at the risk of hurting or displacing themselves). Leader Caregiver will inspire and desire those they lead to be caring and concerned about others promoting and rewarding those who show sacrificial servant-hood first. At the end of the day, the Caregiver might say it was a great day because he or she helped someone and served others sacrificially in a great way, thus enabling others to complete their own life journey.

shade under a large willow tree that looked half-dead. "That was a remarkable plummet you took. Here, let me get some of this debris off your back. And let me carry that backpack."

Setting the backpack on the ground, Caregiver began picking away the twigs and grass Just Middle Manager had gathered during his roll down the incline.

"Thank you for the assistance," Just Middle Manager spoke for the first time. "What happened? One minute I was walking along the path on the valley floor, and the next thing I see is a large log out my peripheral vision. Did I fall over a cliff for real this time?"

"No, you didn't step off a cliff," Caregiver answered, chuckling just briefly but being careful not to hurt Just Middle Manager's feelings by sounding insensitive with the use of humor. "You merely fell into a rut that runs along Victory Valley's floor."

"I fell into a rut?"

"Yes, that is what it is and where you are. Ever so often, those traveling along the road to Celestial City of Influence fall into this rut. But I live here and am more than willing to help you out of it. I can aide you on your way to your destination," Caregiver stated, taking Just Middle Manager's backpack.

He felt a little uncomfortable seeing Caregiver begin to walk on in front of him actually carrying his heavy load, but this was the first time along the entire journey that anyone was willing to carry his pack. When he met Innocent, he was given a sense of hope that made the load seem lighter, but Innocent didn't offer to carry it. With Orphan's warning about the dangers that lie ahead, there was certainly a better sense of balance with the weight, but again, there was no offer from Orphan to carry the freight. And Warrior's words and example of discipline, courage, and tenacity certainly strengthened his back, but Just Middle Manager still left Warrior with the heaviness firmly in place on his own back. Now he watched as Caregiver not only helped him up off the ground, cleaned him up, but also took his load. Within moments Caregiver was stepping up out of the rut and back onto the valley floor, Just Middle Manager's load firmly strapped to shoulder and back.

"How did you know I was on my way to Celestial City of Influence?" Just Middle Manager asked, having many questions to ask Caregiver but not knowing where to start. He also wondered why Caregiver lived in a rut and why anyone would offer to carry another's load?

"I heard you talking with Warrior back there. I am sorry for sounding like I was eavesdropping, but I really was just passing by in the rut below you and heard a small portion of your conversation. I hope you don't think badly of me. Do you?"

"No, of course, I don't think ill of you," Just Middle Manager answered, looking back at the rut they had stepped out of as he came along Caregiver's side. "You have helped me a great deal. If you hadn't come along, I would still be laying their hoping someone would have heard my cry for help. I am fine now. But please, let me carry my own load."

"No, I shall be glad to carry it for you for a mile or two. I can see from the red marks on your neck and shoulders that you have carried the weight long and far. A little rest from the burden will do you good, and I certainly don't mind. I find enjoyment carrying the loads of others."

Insight: Caregiver Leaders might often view problems in regard to how the problem may injure or has injured and/or impeded others. The Caregiver will often provide the nurturing to others to assist them in dealing with the difficulty, possibly even before solving the real problem causing the injury. When solving the source problem, however, Caregivers will often be the ones who do the menial tasks others won't. Personal well-being is not a matter of concern when the Caregiver is in full-service mode, even if the job being done calls for great personal sacrifice.

"Why would one find *enjoyment* carrying the weight of another?" he asked, not wanting to sound egotistical, argumentative, or condescending. He had had enough of that during his conversation with Warrior.

"I am not sure how to answer that question," Caregiver said. "I have never really thought about it. I just do what I do, and I seem to feel better having done it. I have done it so long that I find it natural to do. Does that provide you with a sufficient answer?" Caregiver asked, stopping and turning to face Just Middle Manager for the first time since they had left the rut.

"Yes, the answer is sufficient. It's just that I have already met others on my journey, and none have helped me carry the load. Those I have met have provided some sound counsel for my journey, but you stand alone in regard to practical help."

"I am sure those you have engaged along the way have offered what they needed and what they could," Caregiver stated, sounding more pious than really planned. "What I mean is they no doubt helped you in their own way," he quickly said, trying to balance the undesired piety with the weight of simple observation.

"Yes, I am sure they did," Just Middle Manager responded, feeling a little guilty he had spoken poorly about the others he had met. He felt as though he sounded a little selfish. This was, after all, *his* journey he was traveling and was acted upon by *his* own free will choice. Why would anyone else carry a load he set out to travel with alone? He couldn't believe how easily he let Caregiver bear his load. But more importantly, he couldn't believe how that, in turn, had made him feel as though others should help him as well.

Insight: When Caregiver Leader assists others, that assistance may, at times, actually enable those receiving the help. Those who experience Caregiver's kind acts may begin to take advantage of Caregiver. Hence, since Caregiver finds personal reward and merit in each act of kindness, the more acts of kindness done only means more merit and reward. And so the cycle goes and goes. Worst, those being assisted might become so enabled, they are enticed by a sense of entitlement from others as well.

He felt as though he was not only abusing Caregiver but that Caregiver's act of kindness was enabling him to feel needy. He didn't like the feelings he was having.

"May I have my backpack back?" Just Middle Manager asked, not really wanting the heavy load again on his shoulders but not liking the weight of guilt he was carrying in his heart.

"I shall carry it but a little further, if you don't mind," Caregiver responded, not really looking at Just Middle Manager. "Finder's

Forest is just after the next couple of bends in the path. I would really like to give you a rest from your burden until then. But I will only do so if you don't mind."

The tone in which the question was asked was gentle and full of consideration. Just Middle Manager found it hard to resist Caregiver's charms. *Perhaps just a few more yards,* he thought. *What would it matter*?

They walked along in silence for a while until suddenly Caregiver stumbled on a root sticking up along the path and nearly fell forward from the weight of the backpack.

"Whoa!" Just Middle Manager shouted, assisting Caregiver to gain balance. "I must insist on taking the load back. I can't bear the thought of you carrying it one more step."

"I'm fine," Caregiver snapped back. This sudden and almost angry response caught Just Middle Manager totally off guard. It didn't seem to fit Caregiver's nature, at least not the nature observed thus far.

Insight: Caregiver Leader can get quite possessive of the problems he or she is assigned to or that they may assign to themselves. They may find it hard to give a problem back to others and become defensive if asked or instructed to give it up. Remember their act of kindness is seen to them as the avenue for personal reward. So, Caregiver may feel that if the problem is given away then the act of kindness is no longer needed, and therefore, the personal reward is put on hold at best, or at worse, possibly removed totally.

Adjusting the load, Caregiver picked up the pace, not looking back at Just Middle Manager but focused rather on the road ahead. If there was embarrassment for the sharp change in tone, Caregiver didn't seem to want to portray it, at least not openly.

After a few yards, Caregiver turned back to Just Middle Manager who was simply walking along in silence, and said, "Why don't we stop around the next bend. Earlier I constructed a bench in the shade along the path for travelers. I would think it would be a great place for you to relax."

"And for you," Just Middle Manager stated, hoping Caregiver

would see that the load was shifting to-and-fro and that a break was certainly in order for them both.

"Actually, I'm fine. But you will find the location to be a surprisingly nice place to take a small reprieve," Caregiver responded, ignoring Just Middle Manager's hint that the load had become a burden to carry. "I cleared and constructed this spot for weary travelers like you. From its location, you can see the higher part of the valley where Innocent and Orphan dwell; the richness of Victory Valley, where Warrior resides; and Finder's Forest, where your path must indeed lead you. It offers a panorama of your journey thus far."

Having reached the bench, Just Middle Manager could indeed view the places thus described by Caregiver. It was a grand setting and comfortable as well.

"Oh, look! I can see the rut where you reside," Just Middle Manager stated while pointing back toward where the two had just traveled. Just Middle Manager had noticed that in Caregiver's description of the scenery the rut was left out. He wanted to include Caregiver in the vista and give some recognition to the one who had just carried his load so far.

"I don't really live there," Caregiver said.

"Oh, I thought that is what you said," Just Middle Manager responded back, fully thinking that was what Caregiver had spoken to him earlier. But it was shortly after his fall, so perhaps the bumps from the tumble had caused him to not hear Caregiver accurately.

"Yes, that is what I said, but it is more accurate to say I live in Victory Valley. I find that where I am most needed is in that rut. That seems to be where many travelers are caught on their journey. And since I enjoy assisting them in getting out of the rut and I spend so much time there myself, I sometimes refer to it as my home. But I live in the valley with all its wonderful and victorious rewards."

"Do you and Warrior share in the rewards?"

"Warrior has rewards, well-earned. And I too have some bounty. But, in my opinion, rewards are highly overrated. Also, our recompense for service is earned by much different methods and with, again in my view, entirely different motives. Warrior seems to see assisting others as some kind of competition to be won, but I prefer to simply help out where needed for the sake of helping. Others need to have recognition for what they do, but I prefer to work down in that rut, doing what I can behind the scenes," Caregiver answered, clearly making a point of differentiation between the two of them.

Stretching out on the bench and relaxing a little more, Just Middle Manager asked, "Don't you feel as though you are both very much the same? You both are trying to help others. The methods are different, but the goal the same."

"I suppose you could say that. But, I would be careful not to confuse methods with motives."

Just Middle Manager ignored Caregiver's insinuation that Warrior's motives may be less than honorable and further surveyed the view. He was enjoying that the backpack was off his shoulders but reached up to rub the soreness of his neck and arms. He hadn't realized that the weight was taking such a toll on his body.

Without hesitation, Caregiver stepped behind him and began to massage the neck and shoulder area. Although he felt uncomfortable having someone do such a thing, Just Middle Manager simply relaxed and eased back into Caregiver's gift.

Without stopping the rubdown of his neck, Caregiver asked Just Middle Manager, "Why are you traveling to Celestial City of Influence?"

With his eyes closed and fully leaning back into the kneading of Caregiver's hands, Just Middle Manager answered, "I am traveling to the city in hopes to become Next Great Leader. The weight you have so wonderfully carried for me is not at all supplies, but my personal burden for discovering my leadership style and what actually makes a great leader. As I learn that truth, it is my hope the weight will be gone from my shoulders entirely, and I can arrive at the city worthy enough to wear the name, Next Great Leader, proudly."

"If I were a great leader, I would think that leading has to find a source of strength in serving and helping others," Caregiver stated, offering an opinion but not knowing if it was actually solicited or not.

"I think I agree with you," Just Middle Manager quickly responded, noticing that Caregiver had slowed the massage. He appreciated the insights and wanted Caregiver to know, so he continued by saying, "I think that is excellent advice. But do you think by helping others so willingly and compassionately, they could take advantage of you? I can see that this might be a little bit of the shadowy side of being Caregiver." Shamefully, even as he asked the question, Just Middle Manager didn't pull away from the free massage.

"Taken advantage of? Again, I have never really thought about such a thing. It would seem that those in need would welcome someone to serve, to help, or to care for them. Even those who are not in need would welcome such an attitude in a leader. Don't you think?"

"I am in much agreement with you Caregiver, but wonder, as well, if those being cared for won't fall into a habit of letting others take care of them and never really take care of their own troubles. And if Caregiver is helping others out of the rut, who is helping Caregiver out of the same or a similar rut? Wouldn't it be easy for Caregivers to be so concerned about others that they fail to care for themselves and actually live in the rut?"

Caregiver didn't respond right away to Just Middle Manager's questions but stopped the massage of his shoulders and sat down beside him. Caregiver became very pensive and rehearsed the scene that lay before them both. In the distance they could make out Victory Valley. It looked like the next weary traveler was well on his or her way to being straightened out by Warrior.

"Do you think I am neglecting myself?" Caregiver asked, ending the silence that had grown awkward between them both. The sound in Caregiver's voice was not challenging but rather investigating, as if looking further into a crystal ball that held deeper meaning for life.

"I am only postulating that it could be a possible weakness that could flow as a backwash from the river of strength found in helping others," Just Middle Manager answered. "Think of it as a weakness innate in the strength."

Again there was silence between the two of them for some time, and then suddenly, without comment, Caregiver stood and began to adjust the straps on Just Middle Manager's backpack, making no comment concerning their last dialogue. It was as if Caregiver was comfortable with the strengths of the Caregiver life but didn't want to discuss or think about any shadowy side.

"Caregiver, what are you doing?" Just Middle Manager asked, standing himself.

"I would love to converse with you more, but I believe I heard you tell Warrior you wanted to be off the valley floor before dark. And, indeed, you would be if I did not belabor you with my own thoughts and questions."

"I do not believe you are *belaboring* me at all. In fact, I believe you have given me great insights about leadership and how to adopt your caring nature into my own leadership style."

"I am so glad you were able to gather some benefit from my humble ways and that those life habits could possibly yield benefits to both your journey and your final victory in Celestial City."

"Not only will it aide me in the development of my own style, but I am sure it will yield a great benefit to those I am fortunate to lead. I do believe, if I may say this without offending you, that I would want to be on constant guard of being used by others. I also want to make sure I don't enable others who may need to do things on their own."

"It would seem also that my own personal care and concerns are never neglected. For I fear that one day you, yourself Caregiver, may not be able to make it out of the rut you so sacrificially abide in for the purpose of helping others."

There was no response from Caregiver, but Just Middle Manager did sense that the message was delivered adequately and received clearly. Caregiver simply assisted him by putting the pack back on his back and fine-tuning the straps. Caregiver also ripped a piece of his own garment to create some padding, which Just Middle Manager could place between the straps and the shoulders. When asked what Caregiver would do to replace the torn garment, only a smile was returned. Caregiver seemed to give no concern for what the destruction of the clothing meant personally.

Ready to return to an area of comfort, Caregiver pointed out the best path for Just Middle Manager to take through Finder's Forest. "Be careful that you do not leave the path. For the forest can become mysteriously dark when you wander off the road well traveled. Besides, the path to take to Celestial City of Influence is the one well marked on your map."

After giving a stern warning about Ego and Envy, the two parted ways. But at the edge of the forest, Just Middle Manager watched as Caregiver returned to the rut. Like a child waiting for Christmas morning, Caregiver seemed to be eager to meet the next fallen traveler who fell into that groove. Just Middle Manager could see in the distance that Warrior was finishing with the accosted traveler, who was obviously making a straight path for the furrow. Just Middle Manager wondered if these two were not only the bookends of each other but were also working in concert to obtain additional victories for the valley.

Just Middle Manager turned and headed into the forest. As he walked along the path, the forest darkness made it more and more difficult for him to see the path before him. Without noticing he was drifting to one side, Just Middle Manager slowly began to depart from the path well traveled. With evening approaching quickly, the darkness he began to experience was more than he had planned. He had never thought about darkness until now. Now was not the time to think about darkness. He had no light and could barely see his hand in front of his face. Soon he could see no path and could tell he was getting farther and farther off course. Below his feet there was no cleared lane, but along his knees, he felt both bushes and briers. What was he to do? He knew he had already taken too many steps into the forest and had lost his perspective of where to return to the valley. The darkness caused his map to lose any value, and he suddenly longed for the familiarity of the rut.

Just Middle Manager began to panic, his heart racing, his head darting back and forth, looking for anything that might give him some sense of direction. Suddenly, off in the distance and to the left, he saw what appeared to be a light. It was dim but definitely a light, or so he thought. It was moving toward him. Was someone else in this darkness? If there was someone else, were they friend or foe? He stood frozen as the light approached slowly but deliberately.

Insight Tips for putting *Leader Caregiver* to work in your own Leadership Style - *Successfully*

1 Embrace the act of serving and taking care of those you lead. People will respond to those who not only seem to care about them and their welfare, but actually do something practical to demonstrate that caring. The old adage *that people don't care what you know until they know you care* is an obvious truth every leader should embrace. Serving others is not a real obvious culture commodity in today's macho-lead-from-strength-and-power point of view. But it is a secret strength needed for today's leaders.

2 Be aware that not everyone wants your help and care. You may see them as victims and see them in a way you can alleviate their pain, but they may not want your help. They may be seeking help from others or other sources. Don't feel rejected when they don't succumb to your aide, however. They might know best what they need before you do.

3 Be careful that when you do help others that you don't eventually enable them. Because you are helping them, they may tend to rely upon your help time and time again and never really support themselves. It is easy to help them because you get energy and reward out of the act. But the best help you give them might be that you don't help them at all or that you teach them how to help themselves. Does *if you give a man a fish he will eat for a day, but if you teach him to fish he will eat for a lifetime* make any sense here?

4 Don't neglect yourself. It is easy to hang out in the ruts of life looking for others and forgetting to take care of yourself. Remember you can't help others if you have run yourself out of gas. Taking care of you is perhaps the best way and the first step in taking care of others. You may feel awkward at first taking care of yourself, but over time, you would see that it gives you new energy and new freedom to take care of others.

5 Make sure others know that you are available to help them but you have limits. You have to set your limits and publish them verbally so that others not only know them but will observe them as well. Outlining your personal limits will protect you from abuse, help others to grow without you, and will give you time to recover from past work and service to others.

Words of Adventure and Autonomy from Leader Seeker

The light Just Middle Manager thought he saw had disappeared. He wasn't sure why or how, but the light was gone. *Maybe there was no light,* he thought. Maybe it was just something he was imagining in his frightened state. And he was frightened. He knew he had wandered far from the path and was eager to find it again. At least on the path, he had some comfort. That path had become his safety and security since he began his journey, having left the security of his home in the Village of Followers.

Just Middle Manager had his map, but he couldn't see it. Had he thought to bring a light, he could perhaps locate where he was on the map and find his way back to the trail. He didn't like the feelings that were coming over him. He felt out of control. "Where is that path," he said out loud. His voice echoed in the darkness. The return sound coming back was both gloomy and ghostly.

"Why do you want the path?" A voice behind him asked.

Startled, Just Middle Manager turned quickly to see who or what had just spoken to him. Disappointingly, it was so dark, he saw nothing.

As he peered into what seemed like a black hole before him, the voice repeated its question, "Why do you long for a path?"

"Where are you? Who are you?" he asked, turning left and right quickly, hoping to catch a glimpse of the source of the voice. He wanted to identify if it was a friend for him to embrace or a foe with which to struggle.

"Why don't you just make your own path? You have plenty of

opportunity in front of you to blaze your own trail and make your own personal map," the voice said; the tone and texture of each line was designed to entice Just Middle Manager.

"I can't go where I can't see," Just Middle Manager answered, sounding frustrated. "If I had a light, I would certainly blaze a trail. I would blaze it right back where I came from. But this awful darkness has hindered both movements and progress. Now, I ask again, who are you? And are you one or many?"

"I am Seeker, explorer of the forest and anything else that brings adventure, freedom, and independence. I am alone as most seekers and explorers prefer. Who are you? And why do you long so much for this path you now cry for in the darkness?"

"I don't believe I was *crying* for the path," Just Middle Manager stated. "I was simply longing to return to where I was comfortable and to the course on the map that I am to follow to Celestial City of Influence. I am Just Middle Manager, and I am traveling to Celestial in hopes of having my name changed to Next Great Leader."

"And you hope to accomplish this and to be worthy of such a calling by following the path everyone takes?" Seeker asked, still hidden by the darkness, which Just Middle Manager was still experiencing and struggling to appreciate.

"It is a path I have become fairly familiar with and to my knowledge the only way to Celestial City of Influence. Besides, it matters not what path I take,

Insight: The appetite of a leader following the style of Leader Seeker is about searching out and not conforming to the norms of others. Seeker sees life as consisting of finding places off the regular paths that others follow and blazing his or her own trail, typically alone. The Seeker may view others as selling out to the norms of society in order to be accepted by them. The Seeker's own need to assist others in finding a new path or a new idea gives them their motivation for life. Leader Seeker will inspire and desire those they lead to be inquisitive and adventurous about life, promoting and rewarding those who show a deep desire to step out and be alone with ideas first. At the end of the day, the Seeker might say it was a great day because he or she left society's norms and found a new idea, new place, or a new path others missed.

for in this darkness I can neither see or be seen. Do you have light to offer, or are you content to hide within the darkness? Are you afraid to expose yourself to me? Is something dreadful in your appearance that you fear being made known?" Just Middle Manager asked, hoping to goad or to even insult Seeker into providing some sort of light or guidance.

"You think I am afraid to expose *myself*?" A loud laugh echoed throughout the dark forest. "Since you are the one so stuck to your charted course, I perceived it is you who are afraid to expose yourself!" Seeker continued with a sarcastic tone carrying a clear message. "If you were not so terrified to leave the security of your way, you would have the light you need to find, perhaps, a new or better lane to follow toward your desired destination."

"Why would I leave a path that has served me so well thus far on my journey, Seeker? Why would I not want to cling to the lane that is known and reliable to all as *the* conduit to the place I seek? Besides, on that path, there was at least light to see the steps I would take and the dangers I might meet. But I am now so far from that brightness that I can neither see a danger nor an escape."

"Just Middle Manager, the light is near you. You have but to trust your instincts to see new ways and better avenues to follow. It is not darkness you see but a failure to behold all the new light around you," Seeker spoke, making little sense to Just Middle Manager as the words tumbled into the obscurity surrounding him.

Sensing that Just Middle Manager had not understood, Seeker continued by saying, "You seek what you are familiar with.

Insight: Seeker Leaders might often view problems in regard to how they may present a new opportunity to explore and discover. The Seeker will often use the problem as a chance to visit new thoughts and different lines of reasoning others may miss. When discovering unusual answers to problems, the Seeker may find that they are alone in such solutions however. But the Seeker may not be alarmed by being alone as he or she may relish that position as a new starting point for a new adventure. For the Seeker, every problem is a gate to a new path calling out to them: *follow me, follow me.*

But, by being so stuck to the known, you fail to see the brightest of light that is found in the unknown."

"But I only see darkness. I see no light. A few moments ago, I saw a brief flash of illumination, but it disappeared quickly and is now completely gone. I am not sure I even really noticed anything," Just Middle Manager replied, hoping to discover something by way of light in the darkness. But if there was a darkness that could be felt, this darkness was that type of darkness.

Seeker attempted to clarify his concerns by saying, "When you stepped off *The-Path-All-Do-Trod-And-Travel,* the light you saw for a few moments was that glimpse of some new adventure you felt in your heart and soul. Only a few see it but seldom do; many follow it and continue to behold it. All too often they leave the comfortable and only experience a brief utopia of freshness, and then they scurry quickly back to the same sense of security they experienced prior to their small step of faith into the unknown.

"You are like the others," Seeker continued. "You saw for a brief moment some adventure, then closed your eyes out of fear, and, therefore, missed the very hope you seek on the path."

"You are telling me that I have simply closed my eyes, and that is why it is so dark?" Just Middle Manager asked with contempt in his voice. "I can assure you that I very much have my eyes open and still see only darkness. You are foolish both in your ideas and in your reasoning. I would suspect that you are very much alone, as you say, though I cannot tell since the darkness is so blazing."

"*I am* foolish, you say? Who is standing in perfect light, and who is lost in the darkness of their own mind?" Seeker asked, trying to sound as sarcastic as possible. Then, in more mocking tones, Seeker began to call out to Just Middle Manager from a variety of places in the forest. Like a cruel game of hide-and-seek, Seeker toyed with him until Just Middle Manager finally sat down, dizzy from turning left, right, and all around.

"Why do you tease me thus, Seeker"? He asked, exhausted and embarrassed. He could neither see Seeker nor find his way away from him.

"I do not wish to ridicule you or to cause you any more discomfort," Seeker began to speak, his tone softer and words more measured. "I only wish to have you open your eyes to the freedom that is offered to all those who are willing to leave the comfort of *the* map and seek new lands and new places, off the beaten path. Many travel *the* path and many end up at the same place, but true leaders seek new lands and new horizons. Followers are comfortable with the land of the familiar. They always want to remain on the path of comfort and familiarity. True leaders, on the other hand, seek to find new places and new horizons. If you wish to be Next Great Leader, you can't believe you will accomplish such a worthy task sticking to the same path others are traveling, do you? If you do, don't you think you are not really a leader but just another follower behind some and simply ahead of others?" Seeker concluded the argument with a question, hoping Just Middle Manager could get beyond the darkness of the recognizable and into the light of the mysteries beyond normal vision.

Insight: Those leaders with Seeker styles may view those who are unwilling to travel off the path as lacking courage or character. Since Seekers see the world around them as a place of great exploration, they may be impatient with those who are not as adventurous as they may be and may make fun of their desire to stay in comfortable places, holding to their secure habits.

Seeker stood and watched as Just Middle Manager groped around in his darkness. Having viewed the scene many times and in many forms, Just Middle Manager's plight was not unlike many of those Seeker had assisted in Finder's Forest. Many traveled by this way, hoping to become one thing or another but could never really discover the light of their new life, having been blinded by the habits and contentment of their secure ways. Seeker wondered why they really even entered the Forest. What did they expect to find here? Did they think everything bright and beautiful was along that same one path? Did they think only the best and good of life was found where all could see it easily from the same road? Why did they not enter the place Seeker called home with more insight and desire to open their eyes?

"Please, let me help you," Seeker said to Just Middle Manager, finally finding some mercy by which to help Just Middle Manager in his dark peril.

Quickly clinging to the body he now felt beside him, Just Middle Manager hung on tightly not wanting to let the sturdy frame go. "Thank you! Thank you, so much," he said, easing the grasp he had on Seeker's arm but making sure the arm could still not escape.

"You are more than welcome," Seeker replied, not trying to seek a release from the clutch Just Middle Manager had placed on the arm. Seeker knew it was a necessary part of the process, having been there before. Just Middle Manager obviously hadn't, but Seeker was more than familiar with what had to happen next. Seeker could see the *Y* in the road ahead of them both, but Just Middle Manager was oblivious to it, at least for now. What would happen next would determine Just Middle Manager's future; or so Seeker thought. That was always the thought when the *Y* appeared during this stage of the journey.

"Just Middle Manager," Seeker began. "I am going to try to help you to see the light in which I am abiding. If you believe and try, you too can experience this vast illumination off the charted course. Are you willing?"

"What must I do?" Just Middle Manager asked, still not knowing if he wanted to simply return to the path he had left or walk into this darkness Seeker spoke so grandly about.

"You must first be willing to leave the path you have become so comfortable traveling," Seeker replied, still allowing Just Middle Manager to grip him.

"But that path is the way I am supposed to go to reach Celestial City of Influence," he replied. "Besides, the words spoken to me by Caregiver were to stay strictly on the path."

"Is this the same Caregiver who lives near and in the rut on the valley floor?"

"Yes, it is."

"I would assume that Caregiver, even Warrior, Innocent,

Orphan, and all you may or may not have met would instruct you to stay on the path. They have very little adventure and enlightenment in their lives," Seeker replied, sounding a bit condescending when speaking about the others Just Middle Manager had already met on his journey.

"Yes, I have met them all, and, yes, they have all given me instruction as to the path. Is your insinuation that they are all wrong, and you alone are standing correct?"

"I only tell you that although there are many fine sights and great answers along *the* path; those are not the only sights and answers to be found. I also would add that there are many paths to Celestial City of Influence. Simply because you are off *the* path doesn't mean you are off *all* paths.

"Those you have met may have given you much in the way of insight for your journey, but they have not given you the one thing you seek to get out of your darkness, have they? For, if they have, I encourage you to use the tools they have supplied you," Seeker said, the mocking tone again flowing from the lips. At the same time the mockery arrived, Seeker jerked the security of the arm away from Just Middle Manager.

Again, groping and fumbling in the darkness, Just Middle Manager spoke quickly, "Please, don't leave me here alone. I will consider leaving *the* path. But don't leave me alone. Can't you travel with me through this sea of darkness?"

"No, I can't travel with you nor really help you," Seeker said, withdrawing further away from Just Middle Manager's stretched out and seeking arms. "A real explorer must travel alone. You are searching for something unknown and not yet discovered. Once you are joined by many, you are no longer searching but living in the land of the found."

Just Middle Manager began to feel his way around in the darkness. This time, the aimless groping was with much more deliberate and distinctive movements. "I shall try to forget the path," he said, stopping in his movements as he detected his arm coming across the limb of a tree.

"Great!" Seeker exclaimed, almost startling Just Middle Manager.

"Now," Seeker began again, "you must also be willing to look for something you have never sought or thought about seeking."

"How can one seek something never thought of or previously sought?" Just Middle Manager asked, realizing for the first time he knew very little about seeking and exploring.

"It's not that you are seeking for something you have never thought of. It is that you are willing to explore areas in which you have no familiarity. You are willing to leave the comforts of the known to seek something in the world of the unknown. Take a step in your mind first and then watch, for your feet will then find their footing."

"But don't you think all this exploration is going to take time? Just think how far down *The-Path-All-Do-Trod-And-Travel* I could be right now if I had simply stayed on course?"

"Yes, exploration takes time," Seeker answered. "But time should not be measured in how much distance you travel but by what you experience on the way. If you take time to discover something new, won't that, in time, save you time? When an inventor takes time to try one thing or another and then finally comes up with a great invention that will save others time, does not that make the time he or she took more valuable?"

"Yes, I can see *over time* you could *save time* by seeking. But," Just Middle Manager went on to ask as he fumbled past a rock formation on his left and a tall tree on his right, "isn't there a lot of risk in seeking?"

"There is risk, and loneliness as well," Seeker answered, slowly leading Just Middle Manager around a small hole in the ground that he obviously could not see. "The risk-taking is much easier to handle than being alone. But if you wander off the trail others are holding onto so dearly, you will undoubtedly find yourself alone."

"I am not sure I like taking a risk, and I know I don't like being alone."

"Well, that is the life of a seeker, good and bad."

With those words from Seeker, Just Middle Manager closed his eyes and thought about venturing off into a place he had never before seen or experienced.

As he began to think of a new place or new way of dealing with the problem before him, he noticed a small light once again in the distance. "I think I see something in the distance," he said, almost shouting it out, not realizing Seeker was standing right beside him.

"Is it coming closer?" Seeker asked.

"No, it is not. It is as if it is dancing in the distance, taunting me with its illumination and enlightenment."

"You must be hanging onto something that is forbidding it from approaching and revealing to you the depths of its mysteries."

Just Middle Manager actually took an unconscious step toward the light and unconsciously let the map he was holding slip from his hands. The map was well-worn and tattered by the many steps he had traveled with it gripped by his fingers. But as it slowly hit the ground, the light seemed to rush even closer and brighter than before. Again, without noticing, he took another step toward the light and was actually beginning to walk to one side of the *Y* that was posed before him.

"You are doing just fine now," Seeker spoke, more behind him now than before. Seeker could see that this prodigy was well on his way to the freedom all seekers find. "Just continue to search for that which is unknown and unfamiliar to you. Enjoy the experience you find yourself in, for those on the beaten path do not see what you see or experience what you are now experiencing. And to be a great leader, you must travel new roads yourself before you ask others to be willing to do so."

"But what if I am not prepared for what I see?" Just Middle Manager asked, worried that just as he had not come prepared for the darkness, he might not be prepared for what was about to be revealed in the light he was now beholding.

"Preparation is simply another term for the comfortable life you had in the past," Seeker responded. "To be a true explorer, you cannot really prepare yourself. You must be willing to take on whatever comes with what you have. That is the true excitement found in seeking."

"But it seems foolish to travel into an area and to discover something only to be unprepared for what you find."

"Foolish perhaps but exciting still the same," Seeker answered again with the sound in the voice growing with more and more excitement with every step Just Middle Manager took.

The light that shown now before him was so bright, Just Middle Manager was mesmerized by it and didn't hear Seeker's last comment. What Just Middle Manager now beheld was so beautiful that he could hardly consider the scenery before him.

"What do you see?" Seeker asked.

"You can't see it?"

"No, your exploration has taken you down a path I have never traveled myself. You are actually traveling down a new corridor I have never walked."

"I see a great and beautiful house obviously cared for by someone with much love and passion. It has a large white and inviting gate at the entryway. I see a name on the gate but can't seem to make out what it says from here. The home has tall, white pillars across the front with blue and red shutters outside each of the windows. There is a garden in the front of the home that has equally been cared for. It looks as though it is filled with a variety of delicious looking fruits and vegetables. The home seems to be sitting right on the edge of an overhang with a spectacular view of both Victory Valley and what appears to be a city in the far distance. Could that be Celestial?

"You are correct, Seeker," Just Middle Manager went on to say, now fully engulfed in the light of a noonday sun but obviously still within the midst of *Finder's Forest*. "As I open up my mind to the possibility of something different, new, the light has struck me clearly. I would never have seen such a great place from the path I was once traveling. I am so glad I discovered this new way and was willing to leave *The-Path-All-Do-Trod-And-Travel*.

"You have assisted me in such a great way to discover the

beauty of seeking. Even the load on my back seems less cumbersome to me now," Just Middle Manager added, remembering the load on his back for the very first time since entering Finder's Forest. "Perhaps my leadership style will be less difficult to manage if I include the vision of a seeker?"

"Seeker, are you there? Where are you? Where did you go?" He asked, turning and looking for Seeker for the first time since he regained his focus in the discovery of the newfound light.

He had been so captivated by the sights before him that Just Middle Manager hadn't noticed Seeker was no longer with him. He hadn't noticed that Seeker left him alone at the beginning of the *Y* in the road; the *Y,* that if he would have taken the other way, would have put him straight back on the road to *The-Path-All-Do-Trod-And-Travel.* But now, he didn't even know there was a *Y.*

Just Middle Manager looked for Seeker for a few more moments. He realized there was great strength in the Seeker way but also could clearly see the shadowy side of Seeker. Just Middle Manager made a note of his findings and stuffed it safely into his backpack. He understood that leaving *The-Path-All-Do-Trod-And-Travel* was a risk and might not always have a reward at the end, but it was nevertheless a risk worth taking. He decided he would find a way to emulate the positive aspects of Seeker but to try to avoid the darker sides of such a life. That thought alone gave him more vision and more light. It certainly made his backpack less burdensome.

When Just Middle Manager realized Seeker was gone, he turned back toward the home and garden he had discovered. As he walked up toward the gate in front of the house, the sign above the gate was much clearer and was very easy to read. Carved next to the name on the sign were many small but distinctive hearts. The name on the sign was engraved as well. In big bold letters across the bottom and below the small, distinctive hearts, the sign read *Home Of Lover.*

Insight Tips for putting *Leader Seeker* to work in your own Leadership Style - *Successfully*

1 Embrace the act of searching something out. True Seekers love to find new things and new adventures in problems and in opportunities. Go a different way to work; order something on the menu you haven't ever ordered; take a trip without a map; look at a problem with a completely different frame of view. Looking at a problem in a different way may allow the seeker in you to come away with a new plan, a new method, a new idea, or a new solution. Don't be afraid to try a new approach to an old problem.

2 Remember that true seeking is a lonely job. If you are really going to seek out something new and unthought-of you will certainly be alone in the seeking. You will have times when the loneliness seems scary and dark. But true seeking is fighting through the unknown to discover something or visit something no one else has seen.

3 If you are always seeking, you may not ever be stopping. You can't always be seeking. At some point you have to land in one place, or the seeking you are doing will just be a nice way to cover up the lack of responsibility and the inability to grow up and do something. Seekers have to eventually land somewhere for real meaning to take place. Seeking for the sake of seeking nullifies the value of what you find.

4 If you leave the beaten path all the time and refuse to conform to others or the life around you, be careful that others don't view you as odd and refuse to take you seriously. Because you refuse to conform, others may refuse to listen to your newfound ideas and methods. There is some safety in the beaten path, if only to use it as a conduit for your fresh ideas and thoughts.

5 If you are willing to take a risk and look for new things, you must be careful to realize that you may waste valuable time and it may not work out the way you hoped. To discover new ideas is a risky adventure. Not all new ideas are worthy to explore. You may go down many canyons before you discover an open pass.

Words of Commitment and Passion from Leader Lover

Just Middle Manager wandered around the garden for a brief moment. He hadn't eaten in such a long time. The fruit on the vine seemed to be calling his name. He looked over his shoulder and, not seeing anyone, turned back and began to pick some of the fat red grapes that hung firmly to the vine. They were delicious as they melted in his mouth. Looking again and still not seeing anyone, he took another handful and then began to walk further around the home.

As he reached the back of the cottage, he could see deep into the gorge in front of him. The rocks and forest below looked frozen as though petrified in time. The colors red, blue, and violet reflected off the light illuminating the spot in the forest. As Just Middle Manager beheld the hues, he saw a small rainbow reflecting slightly off a small waterfall. He could see its flow coming off a gorge and into what appeared to be a pond below. It was an amazing scene. A strong feeling of bliss began to flow over his body. *This certainly is one of the places you want to remember and return to time and time again,* he thought.

With a feeling of pleasure coming over him, Just Middle Manager thought of those he had left behind in the Village of the Followers. He had spent much time there and had many friends. He wished they were there to behold what lay before him. Certainly they would be eager to see the sight. *But would they too be willing to get off The-Path-All-Do-Trod-And-Travel,* he thought. *Or, would they be content to simply walk along as clones to the cause and never step into this hidden paradise?*

He took the load off his back, and as he did, the strips of cloth Caregiver had given him fell to the ground. They nestled gently in a bed of daisies that surrounded his feet. As he reached down to secure them, his thoughts of Caregiver caused a smile to come across his face. *This was certainly a place Caregiver would like,* he thought. This was a great place to bring others who were in a rut. It was like a vacationland. Some place you go once a year to relax and recharge.

As Just Middle Manager wandered further around the grounds, he thought it strange that a place so beautiful would not be filled with others. But there was no one. Although maintained with great care and meticulous concern, the residence appeared like a ghost town on a lost map.

"Hello," he called. "Is anyone here? Does anyone live here?"

No answer was heard as he climbed the steps of the porch and approached the front door. To his left was a large and freshly painted porch swing. The cool breeze gently swayed the swing back and forth on its chain link girders. It was as if someone was sitting in the swing and gently swaying it back and forth. It could have been frightening. But it wasn't. Rather, it was inviting and gracious in its appearance.

Just Middle Manager knocked softly on the door. But despite his attempt to squelch the sharpness of the knock by using a gentle tap, the sound seemed to disturb the peace and serenity that had obviously taken a clutch on the surroundings. He knew he was outside, but the feelings he had were the same you would feel as you stepped into the foyer of a very large, but empty church. Noise itself seemed to be a sin.

He waited a few moments after the knock, but when no one answered, he reached for the doorknob. He wouldn't have gone in, he knew, but the desire to enter was so strong he simply wanted to see if he could go through the door if he so desired.

"Hello, there!" A voice behind him invitingly called.

His hand was almost within striking distance of the knob when he heard it. More embarrassed than afraid (for some reason the place left little room for fear), Just Middle Manager turned to see a figure walking past the garden and up the walk before him. Dressed in pure white, the form was obviously of someone who cared for their appearance. As the person approached closer, Just Middle Manager felt a small twinge of escalation. Even though Just Middle Manager didn't know who this was, the smile and warmth generating out before him was so inviting, it was impossible not to think you were in the presence of someone friendly.

"My name is Lover, what is yours, and what brings you to my wonderful abode?" the figure spoke. It was a gentle voice that mirrored both the clothing and the smile that Just Middle Manager saw. The long white robe gently swayed in the breeze as Lover slowly ascended the porch steps.

Just Middle Manager extended his hand for what he thought would be an appropriate handshake as he began to spit out his name, mission, and the destination of his journey. But before he could get half through his response, Lover stepped right through his outstretched arm, past his hand, and put a large embrace around Just Middle Manager's body. It was warm and not at all uncomfortable.

"You are very much welcome here, Just Middle Manager. I thought it might be you. I saw Seeker at the edge of the forest, and he thought you might be coming this way."

"You know Seeker? It was Seeker who led me to this place. Or, at least I think that is what happened. It was so dark for a while that I really am not sure of the events that took place. But I can tell you I am glad to be here. You have a wonderful home. You did say this was your home, didn't you?" Just Middle Manager spoke. He couldn't believe the freedom he felt in Lover's presence. It was as if they had been friends forever and were getting caught up on past events.

"Yes, it is my home, but I doubt if Seeker would have led you here on purpose. Seeker is a person of the open and would refrain from being constrained by even the small fence around my home."

Just Middle Manager looked up and saw a knee-high fence that appeared to circle the entire home, garden, and surrounding area. He marveled that he didn't remember the fence when he first entered into the grounds. *Was it always there, and where did it come from if it wasn't,* he thought. But he was so captured by the sights and ambiance of the home, he could have missed a small fence and even more for that matter.

"I hope you will be staying a while," Lover stated, opening the door of the home and walking through the entryway. "I am sorry I was not here to greet you properly. I was just returning from escorting another traveler to the fence line. She was on her way to Celestial City of Influence. But she was able to stay for some time, and we had such a long and profitable visit. I hated to see her go. I think we created a remarkably strong bond between us in such a very short time. So you too are going to Celestial City?"

Just Middle Manager had followed Lover into the room and missed the question, rather being captivated by the smells, sounds, and sights before him. The music playing in the background was more than soothing. *Like the sound of angel's wings,* he thought. The scent of the room was a fragrance Just Middle Manager could not recall, but he more than liked it. It had a relaxing

Insight: The appetite of a leader following the style of Leader Lover is about creating and maintaining a place and feeling of bliss either for someone or something. Lover is a person of great charisma. Lover sees life in the context of relationships and creates an inviting and accepting atmosphere around them for which to live with others. The Lover may view others objectively at times, but believes all things are solved through love and will seek to create long and bonding relationships. The Lover's desire to fulfill commitments to, and with, those around them motivates them to protect that relationship at all costs. Leader Lover will inspire and desire those they lead to be unified in their concerns and causes promoting and rewarding those who show a deep desire to return love and affection. At the end of the day, the Lover might say it was a great day because he or she established a new relationship, saved a damaged one, or was able to hold onto—through love—a person, occupation, place, hobby, event, or anything that has become the object of their desire.

effect on him, and as a result, he found himself melting into the room rather than walking across the plush carpet beneath his feet.

The most charismatic aspect of the room was the many photos that hung on the walls or sat on tables and dressers around the room. The photos were pictures of many different individuals, people who Just Middle Manager did not know and had obviously never met. But each picture had at least two constants. One consistent aspect was that the background for all the prints showed the photo was taken somewhere on the grounds that Just Middle Manager had just surveyed either outside or inside the home. The other unfailing trait of the photos was that his new friend, Lover, was in each of them. For each individual Just Middle Manager did not know in the captured memories, he could recognize his new friend, Lover, in each. (*But why am I already thinking of Lover as friend,* he thought.) Each of the photographs appeared to carry a special look or convey a unique message; yet, despite the message, he couldn't tell what the meanings were. There was significance contained in each unique frame.

Each picture was placed in strategic places around the room. Some had candles burning brightly near them while others seemed to be purposefully placed in an obscure, dark corner or space. There was not much darkness in the room, but it was obvious these captured memories were placed in the shadowy areas where they were meant to be ambiguous but perhaps not truly forgotten.

Just Middle Manager stared at length at one of the

Insight: Lover Leaders might often view problems in regard to how they affect relationships. The Lover will often use the problem as a chance to build upon a relationship and to make it stronger and/or more committed. When looking for answers to problems, the Lover may view those who are causing the problem as interrupting or damaging a relationship. When this happens, Lover may reject an individual and no longer hold them in such high esteem. The Lover may take on problems personally and view them as an attack to their own beauty, ability, or good will. For the Lover, every problem is the first page of a Hallmark card only needing to be completed with a positive outcome message at the end.

more vague settings. Lover drew near and turned the picture face down. Just Middle Manager looked into Lover's eyes, and it was as if by looking at the photo for so long, Just Middle Manager had brought some pain to Lover.

"Let's move into the dining area, if that is alright with you, Just Middle Manager?" Lover asked, taking him by the arm, escorting him as though the two were walking down an aisle of betrothal. Despite the unusual touch, Just Middle Manager didn't feel uncomfortable around Lover.

"You must be hungry from your long journey," Lover stated, sitting Just Middle Manager down at the head of a very long table.

Lover left the room for a moment but quickly returned with a basket of hot and freshly baked rolls. Again the smell wafted throughout the room and created the mood of goodwill and acceptance. The smell reminded Just Middle Manager of the good times and great meals he had had with family and friends back in Follower Village.

The morose feelings he was experiencing must have shown on his face, for Lover asked, "Do you miss someone special? Is there someone special in your life? You seem to have mentally left the comforts of my home and are away with another."

"I'm sorry. I mean no offense. I have just traveled a long way and find your warmth and inviting nature to be a reminder of those in my own home and town," Just Middle Manager answered, having taken a hot roll from the basket and watching the cold butter melt into its warm craters.

"Those are great memories, and you do well to hold onto them unlike some who go from one person to the next. Having commitment to others is the foundation of life," Lover said, moving a chair closer to Just Middle Manager and taking a roll as well.

"I agree. I do miss those I have left behind. But the destination I travel to will have rewards and relationships as well. Or, so I hope," Just Middle Manager responded, starting to feel a little uncomfortable with Lover taking a seat so close to him when the table before them was obviously large enough to hold many friends and travelers.

"This is a very large table," Just Middle Manager spoke, having washed a small piece of roll down with a glass of red wine Lover had placed in front of him.

"Yes," Lover said in agreement. "I have found amusement and good times with many friends, family, and travelers like you around this table."

"Are the pictures I saw in your sitting room of those you have entertained?" Just Middle Manager asked, wanting to find an explanation for the hundreds of pictures that not only decorated the sitting room but in the dining room they now sat as well.

"Why, yes, they are. I find their memories something dear to hold. Despite my attraction for them, not all share the same sense of commitment and passion that I do, I am afraid," Lover said, turning and looking toward the picture previously turned upon its face.

Just Middle Manager didn't want to pry into Lover's life but was nevertheless curious about the story behind the picture in the frame that was previously marginalized to darkness and now sentenced to face-down time on the tabletop as well. But, the question had to be asked, so he asked it, "Did the individual in that picture do something to hurt you?"

"Hurt is a relative word, isn't it?" Lover asked. But the question asked by Just Middle Manager seemed to cause the hurt within Lover to be exposed with more clarity and to generate turbulence in Lover's face.

Lover asked to be excused and walked out of the room, leaving Just Middle Manager to sit at the table alone. It was the first time during his visit that he had felt awkward. But even by himself at the long oval table, he still didn't feel alone. The awkward feelings really were caused by

Insight: When Lover Leader feels rejected, whether real or imagined, he or she may take the rejection so personal they find it difficult to deal with the individual at the focus of this real or perceived rejection. They may be caught between feelings of moving on without the individual or holding on to the important positive memories they experienced with them. The duplicity of their feelings can cause a severe amount of frustration and/or loss of focus and clarity.

not knowing what to do next, certainly not from abandonment. Somehow, even with Lover out of the room, he could feel the same sense of joy he felt when his host was present.

Curious, he rose from the table and walked over to the double doors opening to a veranda. As he peered through the cut glass windows, he could see the outer edges of the garden he had walked, where he had stolen the sweet fruit earlier. He suddenly felt overly guilty. But even the guilt of stealing from his host didn't seem to sway or derail the warm feelings of rapture he held in his entire being. *What is happening*, he asked himself. *Why am I feeling such a sense of belonging and harmony*?

Just Middle Manager opened the doors and stepped onto the open deck area before him. Looking past the garden, he again saw the fence that surrounded the complex. Still wondering how he may have missed it or passed by it during his entry, he noticed that it was now waist high. *Funny*, he thought, *it was only knee high when I saw it earlier.*

As he began once again to take in the sight and smells of the garden, he suddenly remembered that he had left his backpack on the garden floor in the middle of a flower patch. A sudden feeling of anxiousness began to flow over him. His entire journey was about that pack. But the feelings of bliss and harmony that were now overwhelming him had caused him to completely forget the mission he had embarked upon. He began to stretch his neck up and around the decking to see if he could see his lost possession.

"Are you looking for your backpack?" Lover asked, walking up behind him and carrying a tray of breads, fruits, crackers, and fine cheeses. Not waiting for a response, Lover continued, "I placed it in your room. You will find it secure on top of the bed prepared for you."

"It's in *my* room—a bed"? Just Middle Manager asked, reaching out to take a piece of the cheese being offered to him.

"Why, yes, a room I have prepared for you," Lover answered. "I only assumed you would be staying in my home until at least daybreak. You do not want to return to the darkness of the forest floor, do you?"

"Well, I wouldn't want to impose," Just Middle Manager responded, fully knowing he didn't want to return to any darkness anywhere. Besides, he really liked where he was. There was a sense of love and acceptance in this place, and he wanted to fully embrace it and be embraced by it.

"Come, I would like to show you something," Lover said, taking him by the arm into another room with that same bridegroom-escort walk as before. As they entered, Just Middle Manager could once again see it was filled with mementos and collectibles from the past, again with Lover being a constant theme significantly attached to each object.

"You certainly have an unusual collection," Just Middle Manager spoke, both admiring the items before him but also curious as to their meaning and significance.

"Each of these carries a special meaning for me," Lover spoke as if reading Just Middle Manager's mind. "Take this one, for instance. This is a strap cut from Always Follower upon his return from Celestial City of Influence. We spent days together and have a warm and endearing relationship. I look forward to his return some day."

"Always Follower? He was coming *from* Celestial? What was the purpose of his travel?" Just Middle Manager asked, intrigued by the name.

"Yes, Always Follower," Lover answered. "He was returning from Celestial City of Influence to Follower Village, for he was found lacking. Despite his situation, I found him to be more than a great companion and associate. He became a great friend. He tore one of the outer straps from his pack to leave as a reminder of our bond and his visit."

Placing the strap down once again inside the nook of a well-lighted hutch, Lover made a path around the room showing Just Middle Manager a number of souvenirs of other past visitors who had become glowing friends. Lover told of Often Right who was traveling to Celestial and of Compromise who had also been turned away at the city gates.

Into the night, Lover recounted the sagas of travelers like Dreamer, Looking for Acceptance, Pliable, and Desire to Rule. Each story told was full of expressions of passion and commitment from Lover. Each tale had the theme of casual acquaintance being turned into long-time friend more than a friend—a fellow lover even.

As they discussed Just Middle Manager's expedition, Lover talked deeply and ardently about adopting a leadership style that fostered passion, commitment, and togetherness with others. Lover postulated that a leader who did not show love and commitment to those he or she led was not only a poor leader but deficient at the very core of human emotion and existence. Lover explained the art and importance of embrace whether physically, emotionally, or even ideological.

During their dialogue, Just Middle Manager challenged that Lover and Caregiver were very much the same. He told Lover that he thought Caregiver would enjoy leaving the rut and living in such a home as this. Lover acknowledged the truth of Just Middle Manager's statement only to further explain that the two may have a common theme expressed in their interest in others, but that was the limit of their resemblance. Lover thought that whereas Caregiver wanted to help others, Caregiver also saw everyone as victims to be rescued much like Warrior. On the other hand, Lover's view of others was that they were fellow peers and equals, someone to enjoy through relationship and union.

Having spent the majority of the night in deep discussion, Lover hinted that rest was in order and escorted Just Middle Manager to a room on the second floor of the home. Like the rest of the house, the room was not only inviting but full of memories and the signs of lasting friendships. Although not large, the room was more than comfortable in size. In the center of the room was a bed that looked more like it was prepared for intimacy than a simple night's rest. Just Middle Manager stood in the doorway for a few moments not sure whether he wanted to enter.

"Please, come in and find some comfort," Lover stated, sensing

Just Middle Manager's loss of ease. "There is little to fear here. I only wish to make your stay as appealing as it is practical. You will be alone and no one—I assure you—will invade your privacy or make you feel uncomfortable."

"I just really feel as though I am imposing on you, Lover," he said as he walked past the bed to the window, looking up into the night sky. A full moon had replaced the light he remembered from earlier. Looking down and using the moon's rays as a guide, he once again could see the fence that surrounded the garden and the home. Now, as he beheld it, he knew something was different. This time the fence was chest high. There was something happening, and he was struggling with the meaning.

Insight: Because of the bliss and the desire to make others comfortable, Lover may at times need to establish well-defined and informed boundaries. Those with the Lover style are not afraid to get close to others they meet and lead. As a result, they may, at times, cross the line with inappropriate innuendo or even actual behavior. The establishment of boundaries, meaning, or intent is always a proper strategy for Lover.

"What about this fence you have around the house?" Just Middle Manager asked, feeling rather blunt but seeking a practical explanation to a question that now seemed important to him.

"Well, first, this is a home not merely a house. And, as to the fence, we shall talk about that at breakfast, my friend," Lover said and quietly slipped out the door, closing it and latching it simultaneously.

As Just Middle Manager laid his head on the bed and into the softness of the pillows, the fragrance and mood of the home seemed to engulf him. Within moments he was lost to anything around him. Little did he know the next morning the mood and tone of the entire home would change with the discussion of the fence and what it meant to him and others who had traveled through this place.

"So you were going to tell me about the fence surrounding your compound?" Just Middle Manager asked, taking another sip of coffee and enjoying the large spread of breakfast food in front of him. Again, he felt both cared for and important in Lover's home. He would have ignored the chain-linked wall if it wasn't for the fact he noticed upon his waking that the top of the fence was now eye level. For the first time, Just Middle Manager noticed the fence was not actually on the outside of the garden but almost appeared as though it were part of the plants.

"You ask so many questions," Lover responded, diverting the question somewhat by offering Just Middle Manager another serving of fruit, apparently freshly picked that morning.

"Well, it's just I have many steps to travel today and must get on my way. Yet upon surveying your fence, I see no opening. It is as if the entire compound is enclosed by it. What is the meaning of such a large barrier? And, I sense it almost growing as though it were alive and part of the plot you live in," Just Middle Manager said, finally getting into discussing the very thing that was on his mind.

"Well, if you must know," Lover began, a soft tone being replaced by a matter-of-fact delivery. "Unlike Seeker, who seeks the hills and forest for something new, I, Lover, find security in that which is good and established. As I find a great relationship, it is my desire to keep it and to cultivate it. As a fence is the nemesis of the Seeker, it is the ally of the Lover."

Insight: The Lover style is to embrace and hold onto things important to them. The Lover can have a difficult time letting go of something or someone, allowing them to seek their freedom. The Lover may interpret another's desire for freedom and adventure as abandonment and loss for them personally. Hence they tend to create locking fences around those they lead and expect loyalty within the compound they have created rather than beyond it.

"I sense your meaning but also see your tone has changed toward me," Just Middle Manager stated.

Lover sat for a moment in silence and then finally said, "I do not wish to have our relationship damaged by my desire to hold onto what we have built together. If you must go, then you must go."

Just Middle Manager spoke quickly, almost cutting off Lover's words. "But, we really haven't built anything. We have only been acquaintances for a brief time." Just Middle Manager could see he was being looked upon as another person in Lover's life that had suddenly become closer than Just Middle Manager had intended.

"What I mean is," Just Middle Manager continued, "you have taught me something I had not considered in my journey to become Next Great Leader. I see how important it is to communicate proper feelings and how a great leader will form bonds with those they lead. You have also taught me the importance of spreading that love through those who follow. But I must still be able to complete my quest, for that is what brought me here and must in turn send me away. I perceive your strength of building relationships, although love can also hinder you in your ability to let go of those you love so deeply."

"Yes, I can see that," Lover answered, finding some solace in the fact that their conversations had led to Just Middle Manager's growth and maturity. "But before you go, could we get a picture together for my mantle? I shall so cherish our time. I have just the perfect place for it in the sitting room."

As they completed the taking of the photo and talked briefly about the path from Lover's home to Celestial City of Influence, Lover escorted Just Middle Manager out of the home and to the edge of the compound. Although he had not seen it earlier, Just Middle Manager indeed saw a gate in the fence. The fence didn't seem as tall as it did earlier, and somehow he knew it would slowly slip back into the ground the farther he traveled from the home. But Just Middle Manager could certainly see why Lover wanted to stay close to such a place.

He made a note that holding onto something or someone was a good thing for a leader to do, but it may also limit the ability to find the new horizons Seeker had previously taught him. Together, he knew that the two of them taught him some valuable lessons about leadership style. As he made a mental note of Seeker's advice to leave the path for something new and Lover's warmth of holding onto relationships of the past, his load lifted slightly. It no longer hung so heavily on his shoulders, and it was a good thing; for when he parted ways with Lover, Just Middle Manager too left something to be remembered by. He felt a little guilty for doing so since the object left for Lover wasn't actually Just Middle Manager's. Despite not really being his, it still held meaning for Lover in that way. Just Middle Manager hoped Caregiver would never travel out of the rut and into Lover's home. For if that happened, then Caregiver would see that lying quietly alongside the picture of Just Middle Manager and Lover were two strips of cloth formally torn from Caregiver's garment.

Upon leaving, Lover had placed something in his bag. Just Middle Manager knew what it would be. It would be a picture of the two of them standing in front of the row of grapes he had stolen and eaten from the day before. He assumed it was Lover's way of saying that he was forgiven and that love cures all.

Insight Tips for putting *Leader Lover* to work in your own Leadership Style - *Successfully*

1	Make commitments. Don't be afraid to commit to something. It will balance the Seeker in you and will allow others to see that you are invested in people, the project, or mission of the team.
2	Don't hold on so tight to those in your life that they can't breathe. A warm embrace is always nice, especially on a cold day or in a bad situation. But you can embrace for too long and too hard, smothering the very person for which you have love or concern. Don't allow your love for them to become an enclosed fence around their lives.
3	Don't be afraid to embrace someone; if not physically, then emotionally or even spiritually. People have a large hole in their lives that can only be filled by other people. There is a reason that when people breakup with someone in marriage or friendship most find someone else. It is in the human DNA to love and be loved. Embrace it!
4	Make sure you establish boundaries in your life so you don't fall into the tendency of the Lover to be promiscuous or inappropriate. You can create a warm mood and a warm environment, but you can't cross the line and do something inappropriate because the mood or environment made it easy. Moods should be just moods, not diving boards into improper indulgence.
5	Love can solve any issue, but you still have to find a functional and practical method by which to do so. The *feeling* of love is not a replacement for the *action* of love. Find ways to be practical without sacrificing your desire to love others and be loved by them.

Words of Metamorphosis and Revolution from Leader Destroyer

Destroyer walked carefully along the bottom of the precipice and watched the weary traveler take his final push off the last rung of the ladder and back over the edge. As each dejected rung returned the traveler to the top of the cliff, Destroyer was shown this was just another average explorer. He may have had good intentions of making it to and through Celestial City of Influence, but he never would.

Destroyer wondered why this voyager couldn't complete such a small step on so great a mission. Celestial City of Influence was clearly visible from this point on the journey. It was foolish to have your hope so close and not be willing to finish off one small step. It would have put him that much closer to his desired destination. Undoubtedly, the visit with Innocent had encouraged this traveler enough with anticipation to get him this far, and Destroyer could tell that the traveler was well equipped concerning the warnings from Orphan to make it through both the valley and to this point in the forest, avoiding the pitfalls most don't.

As Destroyer paced along the ravine floor, it was clear that it wasn't the optimism of Innocent or the forgetting of the warnings of Orphan that held this poor traveler back, nor was it the competitive nature or will to act, obviously learned from Warrior, that prevented him from moving closer to his beloved goal. And, although the helping character of Caregiver and the investigative nature of Seeker may have given the traveler pause, it wasn't their advice, counsel, or personality that prevented him from climbing down this rock face. No, for this traveler it was the grip of Lover that he could not shake. Had he been willing to leave the memories, emotion and ambiance of Lover, he may have been able to get through this one last step. Destroyer knew that this traveler had mistaken the simple aura and feelings of Lover's moods with the reality of holding on to what is truly valuable and worth cherishing. But upon his return to Lover, he would soon find the fence up and the mood gone. Most do.

But it didn't matter much to Destroyer. There would be more foolish hikers along the way, hoping to have their wishes met and expectations delivered in the City. But the path for this one traveler ended with broken dreams. This one, bearing the name Leader of Many, was anything but that. He was just another poor and naïve traveler who would never see Celestial City of Influence. He, like most, thought climbing the ladder of success meant it was always going up. But Destroyer knew that to be a true leader there is often a need to go down and to make needed sacrifices. Most could not descend to Destroyer's level of commitment. Who would be the next weary soul to fail?

Destroyer took a seat on an all-too-familiar log that allowed head and back to actually rest against the rock face. It would be difficult for anyone to see Destroyer from above, but it was the most comfortable place to patiently wait for another traveler. It would not be long now. For just above Destroyer, coming to the edge of the precipice, was the next hopeful voyager. This one, Destroyer had been informed, was Just Middle Manager. The report was that he was a likeable fellow and, like Leader of Many, was another eager traveler from Follower Village, just like all the rest.

As Just Middle Manager reached the edge of the cliff, he obviously could not see Destroyer at the bottom of the drop off, but he had come to the conclusion he was not alone. He had come to realize with each of these engaging acquaintances along the way, he had plenty of company on this trip. But when Leader of Many stuck his head up over the edge, from seemingly nowhere, he was more than startled.

"Whoa! Let me help you," Just Middle Manager said, offering a hand and pulling as hard as he could. To the casual observer, it may have appeared as though he was actually lifting Leader of Many to his rescue. He wasn't. Just Middle Manager was just offering a hand—*something Caregiver would be proud of,* he thought.

"Thank you. I appreciate the help," Leader of Many said as he wiped clear the dirt and dust he had gathered from pulling himself up the worn rope ladder.

"Where exactly did you come from?" Just Middle Manager asked, still not real comfortable around the edges of a cliff but nevertheless leaning slightly over the edge to discover the answer to his own question. *Orphan would be pleased with my caution,* he thought to himself.

"Where I came from was down there," Leader of Many answered, somewhat with an angry tone. "And where I am going is back there," pointing back to the path Just Middle Manager had just trod.

Just Middle Manager kept staring down at the ravine below. *Is that someone sitting down there*? Then he turned his eyes back down the footpath he had just walked. More than once, he had thought about turning around and returning to Lover's home, but both his will and his mission would not allow it.

"That is a grand path to follow," Just Middle Manager spoke first, breaking the silence between them. They both had stared for a moment looking over the edge and then back again toward Lover's home.

"It is not the path I long for," Leader of Many answered, his angry tone converting to more desire and anticipation. "I long for the companionship and camaraderie of one I met up the path earlier."

"Was it Lover?" Just Middle Manager asked, knowing full well the answer.

Leader of Many turned from his longing gaze toward Lover's home and back to Just Middle Manager and said, "Yes, do you know Lover?"

"Yes, I do."

"I long for those feelings I had of harmony and friendship. So I am returning to that place."

Just Middle Manager paused for a moment and then said, "Returning? Where were you going that you find it now necessary to return?"

"I was desirous to go to Celestial City of Influence to become Next Great Leader, but the fool at the bottom of this cliff turned me back."

"Fool?" Just Middle Manager asked. "Who are you referring to?" He again looked over the edge to investigate the shadow he thought he noticed earlier.

"If you proceed down that impossible and faulty staircase and get to the bottom, you will learn soon enough who I refer to," Leader of Many said, already hurrying down the path as though back over the edge of the cliff there was a rare disease or plague he wanted to avoid.

Just Middle Manager watched as he hurried down the path. It was difficult for him to watch another make strides toward Lover's home. He, himself, wanted to return to the bliss and wonder he too had felt there. But Just Middle Manager remembered the words of Seeker about finding new paths and discovering wonders outside the norm. Looking back over the edge of the cliff, Just Middle Manager knew he had discovered one of those new places.

Looking cautiously over the edge again, Just Middle Manager wondered why he wasn't as terrified as when Orphan had tugged him back from a near demise. Perhaps the courage, spirit of action, and competitive nature gathered from his talk with Warrior had given him a sense of strength and determination, or at least, that is what he was hoping his mind would imagine.

Finally, after using his new Seeker ways and looking for other possible paths to proceed to Celestial City of Influence and finding none, Just Middle Manager called down over the cliff and into the ravine. Although he still saw no one, Leader of Many's words gave him hope someone, fool or not, was below and would respond with some instruction. He had determined not to go back, and there was no other way but down. This confused Just Middle Manager somewhat. *Why, if I am to lead, must I go down? I thought leadership was about climbing up the ladder of success and not about going down?*

"Hello, is there anyone down there? Is anyone there who can give me some advice as to how to descend to the bottom? I wish to make my way to Celestial City of Influence and become Next Great Leader. My name is Just Middle Manager, and I am prepared to do what I must do to get to my desired goal."

As Destroyer sat and listened to the voice coming from above, it was difficult to contain the chuckle of humor that was boiling up inside. *So, this traveler is "willing to do what he must do."* This thought brought a smile to Destroyer's face. But, nevertheless, for the sake of common sense, the humor was capped off, and Destroyer called back, "Yes, someone is here. State your business and your need."

"I would like to descend down the face. But I don't seem to know how to accomplish this," Just Middle Manager shouted back down into the ravine while trying to locate the source of the response.

"Simply ask the one you just assisted over the edge. Certainly he has a tale to tell and can assist you. Then again, be leery of his narrative as I have found him somewhat lacking in substance."

"He has already departed back down the path toward—"

"Toward Lover's home?"

Insight: The appetite of a leader following the style of Leader Destroyer is about moving on and letting go. Destroyer sees life as a balance between working with that which should be destroyed and with that which can be salvaged, before it destroys too much. The Destroyer may view others as someone to hold on to (salvage) or to cut lose (destroy). The Destroyer's desire to let go and move on motivates their behaviors. Leader Destroyer will inspire and desire those they lead to be useful and calculating in their work promoting and rewarding those who don't waste time on unvaluable activities and make good decisions about moving on with a willingness to fix what they can and disregard what they can't. At the end of the day, the Destroyer might say it was a great day because it was revolutionary; he or she let go of something that was wasteful and made way for something that was not.

Destroyer shouted, ending Just Middle Manager's sentence for him. "Typical. I could have predicted that. He was neither worthy of my help or Celestial's, for that matter." Just Middle Manager found Destroyer's words and tone coarse and out of suit with the experience he had just enjoyed with Lover. He wondered if Leader of Many had the same struggle. *Perhaps the difficulty in making the transition to the bottom was not a physical one,* he thought, *but a relational one*?

"Yes, that is where he said he was going. But, I am not he and would like to descend to the bottom as I see this as the only way to Celestial. What must I do?" Just Middle Manager asked, desiring to prove himself to this voice in the narrow valley below. "Also, why must I go down to get to my desired location?" He asked, hoping the *fool* at the bottom would give him some needed and necessary motivation for the apparent steep descent.

"Sometimes you have to go down before you can go up," Destroyer said, responding to the last question before the first. "Your fellow traveler, like many from your village, could not make the final descent. Are you as equally challenged?"

"I am only challenged as to reason not by will!" Just Middle Manager called back, sounding as strong in tone as he felt in brawn and will.

"Then simply begin your plunge. Use the rope ladder at your feet. But be advised; each rung on the ladder has a special meaning and need. You cannot pass over one without the other, and you must let go of the one before the next can be fully utilized."

"Are you saying I must let go of the first before I can step onto the second and let go of the second before I can step onto the third and so on?" Just Middle Manager asked, not wanting to consider such a descent. "This approach doesn't sound very plausible ... much less safe!"

"You must first let go of your fears, and then you will be able to take each rung on its own merit. Didn't you learn anything from Seeker? Are you still blinded by the darkness of your own ignorance?"

Remembering both the difficulty surrounding the darkness in the forest as well as the benefits that yielded, Just Middle Manager gathered his courage and reached down to seize the first rung of the ladder. Lifting it to create a better position, he could read an inscription across the first step. The message carved into the wooden rung was obviously engraved by someone who had skill with a knife. It read, *Sometimes You Just Have to Let Go.*

"I am not so sure such a message is wise for the first rung of a ladder or for any rung on a ladder for that matter," Just Middle Manager called down toward Destroyer, who had left his log perch and was now standing in clear view.

"Do you think letting go of a ladder at this height would be a wise thing to do?" he called out again not getting any response from the first statements.

"You don't have to climb down. You can go back to where you came from. You will have plenty of company," Destroyer yelled back. "Assuming you only had to show up at Celestial City of Influence for a new title isn't leadership. That's entitlement. You have to prove to yourself you have what it takes to become Next Great Leader," Destroyer continued.

Insight: Destroyer Leaders might often view problems in regard to how they can be survived or not survived. The Destroyer will often view the problem in regard to salvage-ability, preferring to cut their losses sooner than later. When looking for answers to problems, the Destroyer may, at first, become angry and look to throw the baby out with the bathwater, eventually salvaging what they can. When this happens, Destroyer may dismiss individuals who they perceive were a cause of the problem and view them as unneeded or unuseful.

Just Middle Manager would have jumped full bore into a discussion as to how Destroyer knew so much about him, but he was too engaged in getting himself down the side of the cliff face. He would investigate Destroyer's apparent omniscience at the bottom … if he made it to the bottom.

As he made his way down the rungs, Just Middle Manager could see that the handmade steps had received great care concerning their construction. Each rung carried a specific message.

The second rung was engraved with *You Can't Hang on Forever.* The third and fourth had a combined message that read *Things Can Lose Their Value; Don't Hold onto Them Forever.*

Just Middle Manager could see that every rung's message centered upon one specific theme: making the sacrifice to let go and moving forward. It was as though he was being taught some life philosophy by this measured and calculated medium.

Just Middle Manager understood the messages and did get their meanings. That was not the difficult portion of this test. The complexity he faced now was unlike descending a normal ladder. For with this ladder each of the rungs became farther and farther apart. Even a long-legged man would have difficulty making his way up or down, especially as he reached the last two rungs.

To make matters worse, as Just Middle Manager looked past the last rung, he could see that the end of the ladder was still a good measure off the ground. Even if he could touch the last rung, how was he to get to the ground? Maybe there was a reason Leader of Many had climbed back over the top of the cliff's edge?

Now stuck holding one rung with his hands and barely touching the last, Just Middle Manager was somewhat suspended in midair. He could get the balls of his feet onto the last rung but felt completely out of balance between the two. He certainly wasn't willing to let go of the one he held firmly in his hands. The message on that rung, now hidden by his tight and growing-red fingers, read *Cut Your Losses.* He didn't know what the message on the last rung would tell him, but he was certain he wouldn't be letting go. That was out of the question.

"Are you just going to hang there?" Destroyer asked, now plainly visible to Just Middle Manager. Destroyer looked much like an average hunter. The one distinguishing item was not the face, body, or dress, unfortunately. The one thing Just Middle Manager noticed about Destroyer was the very large knife scabbard at the side.

"I am not sure I really want to let go of this rung with my hands when the next is not really secure to my feet. And the drop is certainly far enough one could be severely injured."

"Well then, start pulling yourself back up," Destroyer said, the sound of disappointment very much heard. "But I really thought you had what it takes to get beyond the last rung," Destroyer said, moving back toward the log, which had been a home for many hours, days, and even weeks.

"Wait!" Just Middle Manager called seeing Destroyer walking away. "Can't you help me here? If I let go, I am not certain that I will be able to land safely on the next rung. Your earlier instructions might have been good when the rungs were closer together, but this last rung is a far distance. What does the last rung say, anyhow?"

"What difference does it make what the last rung says? If you aren't going to make it to the last rung, you don't need to know what it says."

"Perhaps if I knew what it says, it would give me some motivation to '*Cut Your Losses*!'" Just Middle Manager responded, getting tired of both hanging by the ladder and of this learning-by-rung approach.

"The last rung says *Just Move On*," Destroyer said, stopping the retreat toward the log chair and returning to stand almost directly under Just Middle Manager. "Why don't you try to get a balance between the two?" Destroyer continued, still hoping that Just Middle Manager could make it.

"There must be a lesson to learn here?" Just Middle Manager asked. "I gather part of leadership is learning to *cut your losses* and *just move on*."

"Actually, if you can strike the perfect balance between the two, you are well on your way to Celestial City of Influence," Destroyer said, guarding the hope heard in Just Middle Manager's reasoning. Destroyer had come to realize that a number of individuals could make the intellectual ascent to such a theory but only few ever really made it to the practical side of letting go and moving on.

Just Middle Manager thought through the dilemma before him. To go back was enticing, and if this was the reason Leader of Many had returned to Lover's home, he felt badly that he had made such a sarcastic judgment toward him.

But Leader of Many was not his concern. Just Middle Manager had to make his own decision. Fortunately, he knew it wasn't really a decision he had to make. For the decision to *Cut Your Losses* was made prior, many steps up the path. Indeed, he was trapped by the thought of *Just Moving On*. It was then that he learned what he hoped was the secret of Destroyer.

"Is this my lesson: That a good leader needs to know when to cut his losses and just move on?" Just Middle Manager asked, thinking he had learned the purpose of this portion of his journey. He wanted to show Destroyer he was both teachable and knowledgeable. He felt a sudden large feeling of pride within his heart, and that he was, perhaps, finally proving himself worthy of Celestial City of Influence. He couldn't help but smile with his chest filling with arrogance.

As his upper body filled with the air of self, it slowly began to push Just Middle Manager farther away from the rung he so tightly held. The prideful notice of his own progress, both physically and mentally, had caused his hands to slip from *Cut Your Losses*. Worse, his feet entirely missed *Just Move On*. As a result, his body, like a rock, fell to the ravine floor. Along with the sudden sound of impact, a large cloud of dust flew up engulfing both himself and Destroyer, who could not move out of the way fast enough. Fortunately, he landed on the backpack, which absorbed most of the shock. But the fall had caused him to be less concerned about the pack and more about his leg severely twisted under him.

Insight: The Destroyer may be the best style to incorporate in the dealing of self and too much pride. Learning to let go of anything is hard, but learning to let go of self-assurance and trusting in one's own strength and talent may be the biggest challenge for a leader. Destroyer can assist in the process of letting go of self and creating more appropriate things to hold to for strength and success. Most leaders are brought down by their own ego when they are filled too much of self and can't let it go.

"I see you have not heeded the advice you have received about

Ego!" Destroyer said, looking down at Just Middle Manager, the sound of laughter filling the ravine.

"Actually, I have received little advice about Ego. Only that along with Ego, Envy travels as well," Just Middle Manager spoke with much difficulty, most of the air in his lungs having left with the thud he heard echo against the cliff wall.

"Well, then heed this guidance, my friend," Destroyer said. "If you want to make your way to Celestial City of Influence, you shall have to make sure Ego doesn't sneak up on you like it just did! Next time the fall from self could be fatal. Many leaders have failed to heed such counsel and fallen to their deaths."

"I am not sure it was Ego that caused my fall but a mere indiscretion of the hand," Just Middle Manager said. Yet, Just Middle Manager knew full well that had he not felt so proud, he would still be holding on to the rung above.

"Besides, I am here, aren't I?" he asked, the air returning to his lungs. He picked himself up from the ground and asked, "Where is here, anyhow?" As he looked around, he simultaneously began to look at and care for the injury to his leg. He wished Caregiver were somehow present in this place.

Destroyer watched as Just Middle Manager began to mind his leg. The discomfort caused by the fall was obvious.

"You are in the Ravine of Recovery. It is a small but meaningful ravine of Finder's Forest," Destroyer said, ignoring Just Middle Manager's clear pain. "Most leaders don't make it here because they hang on to their bad ideas and their false beliefs as to what is valuable for so long before they learn to—"

"'*Just Cut Your Losses*' and '*Just Move On*!' Yes, I got it." Just Middle Manager jumped in, completing Destroyer's sentence. Quickly he looked around to make sure there was no sign of Ego.

"Yes, that is correct. Most leaders never learn to let go."

"The *Ravine of Recovery?* How is it so named?" Just Middle Manager asked feeling as though the dialogue would be good for them both.

Destroyer went on instructing Just Middle Manager in the fine art and responsibility of letting go and moving on. Just Middle Manager nodded approvingly as he was told how those that don't let go can never recover and never really move on to a revolutionary time in their lives. Destroyer explained that before you can have something that is new and energizing, you may have to let go of something that is warm, comfortable, and enjoyable but has lost its vigor.

"So," Just Middle Manager asked, "Leader of Many was not only returning to Lover, but he was doing so on the Road to Ruin? For if you find you can't let go of that which may no longer be productive in your life (and, perhaps, may have become destructive), it may eventually bring you down as well."

"Yes, this is the thought," Destroyer said, leaning back against the face of the cliff and sitting comfortably back on the log.

"But Destroyer—and forgive me if my speech is too forthright—I perceived that you are somewhat coarse in your manner and cutting in your approach. Do you not see you may fall into a position of anger and be too quick to let go? I cannot believe that my fall from such a height is a good thing for me. In fact, as I continue to walk, I perceive that this hitch in my gait will not be gone quickly. Do you not think it harsh to make the rungs so difficult and to build a ladder that is much too short for its purpose?"

Destroyer didn't respond right away to the charges made by a very sore Just Middle Manager. But after they had discussed it further, they both agreed that this was Destroyer's shadow side and that a good leader would do well to know both Destroyer's strengths (learning to let go and to move on) and the darker side (the danger of letting go too soon and of producing a destructive tendency as a result).

As Just Middle Manager made his way up the path toward Celestial City of Influence, Destroyer walked slowly beside him. The limp in his walk caused Just Middle Manager much pain, but they both thought this scare was a good lesson about letting go too soon and about Ego.

"You should learn to cherish the limp," Destroyer commented.

"Before I move on, Destroyer, may I ask you one last question? And, again, I ask without wanting to sound too outspoken."

"Of course you can. But this is about as far as I can go with you," Destroyer responded.

Their walk had brought them to the end of the ravine and to the bank of a wide river. The sound of the water flowing so freely seemed to call to Just Middle Manager. Beyond the river, on the opposite side of the flow, was Celestial City of Influence. It would have been easy for him to move quickly on since his destination was so close, but Just Middle Manager needed to know one more thing.

"Why don't you?" he asked Destroyer.

"Why don't I what?" Destroyer asked in return, confused by the partial question.

"Why don't you *Just Move On*? Why do you stay here in this ravine? You seem to violate the very lesson your ladder wishes to teach," Just Middle Manager said, seeing that his observations were difficult for Destroyer.

"Why don't we just say that is also part of my *shadowy* side, as you refer to it," Destroyer said, withdrawing and heading back up the ravine. "Perhaps, alone I am incapable of really moving on? Perhaps my partner could help me complete the revolutionary process?"

"Partner?" Just Middle Manager asked. But, there was no response. Destroyer just continued the walk back toward the log that had obviously become home. Soon another traveler would come by, and the cycle of training would begin. *But will Destroyer ever let go of the ravine and move on*?

Just Middle Manager contemplated why Destroyer was stuck in one spot and assumed that it would be difficult to move on if you are only focused on the letting go. Destroyer seemed to be focused *only* on letting go. Perhaps, the strength of Destroyer had also become the weakness: If you focus too long on just the letting-go part, you may never have time or energy to complete the revolution by creating something new.

Just Middle Manager didn't know how important that truth was, but he was about to learn a valuable lesson concerning its mystery ... from Destroyer's partner. For, just as he approached the bend in the road, he heard a faint explosion. Suddenly, the river to his right began to flow completely over the path and cut off his trail. Before and behind him, the river began to rise, slowly stealing away any dry ground in its path. Before he knew it, Just Middle Manager was completely surrounded by water. Celestial City of Influence was directly in front of him, but he was separated by the river flowing not only over its banks but beginning to swallow his little island as well. If there ever was a time to just cut your losses and move on, this was it. But where could he move on to?

Insight Tips for putting *Leader Destroyer* to work in your own Leadership Style - *Successfully*

1 Learn when not to let go. Not everything or everyone you have held for years will continue to provide the same sense of security, enthusiasm, or excitement. But that doesn't mean you have to let it or them go completely. The reason the grass looks greener on the other side may be because you haven't watered your own side.

2 Learn how to let go. If you become really skilled with a knife, you might be able to carve well and cut even better. But cutting and carving tend to leave their marks. Careless butchers can often lose a finger before they cut their last piece of beef. Don't make a mistake with the knife. Cut carefully and surely lest you injure yourself and others.

3 Learn when to let go. Be measured in your response to end something. Moving on for the sake of moving on isn't a great philosophy. Let go gently and remember others may not be ready to move on. You may have to give them a ride on the bus and let them see some of the sights before they really want to move completely.

4 Calculate the pain of letting go. Don't let go blindly. Remember that it might hurt you and will certainly hurt others. Knowing the pain of letting go doesn't make it any easier or more comfortable. It doesn't even make it more predictable. It might make it more tolerable, however.

5 Learn to live with the scars. Letting go often leaves a long-lasting scar. Scars are usually something we hide because they are embarrassing or just plain ugly. But come to realize the scar is also a great reminder of lessons learned and times not so good. A scar is nature's tattoo of the meaning and lessons of life.

Words of Creativity and Imagination from Leader Creator

Insight: The appetite of a leader following the style of Leader Creator is about imagination and the fulfillment of it. Creator sees life as a canvas and looks to spread paint in a variety of ways to catch an unfamiliar look or shape. The Creator may view others as mere objects and mediums in the designs they have for their life. The Creator's desire for the vision of new and improved ways to do things motivates their behaviors. Leader Creator will challenge and inspire with vision those they lead to be as equally creative in their work, promoting and rewarding those who come up with innovative ideas and plans (they may not work or ever be implemented; the coming up with the idea might be reward enough). At the end of the day, the Creator might say it was a great day because it was visionary; he or she was able to see or create something concrete or, better, develop something stable and tangible.

"Sorry, my friend, I had imagined this all would have turned out better. Are you okay? Do you think you can get to safety?" a mad-scientist-like figure called out, yelling from across the river. Standing on dry land, slightly down from the gates to Celestial City of Influence, Just Middle Manager could see someone in an obviously torn and tattered white coat. The dilapidated state of the white coat testified to only barely surviving the minor explosion.

"I am okay, but for some reason, the river is trying to swallow me alive," Just Middle Manager called back, becoming more and more frantic as the flowing water decreased his dry island to what seemed to him the size of a postage stamp. Since he could not swim, the height of his panic was rising faster than the water levels. The torrent of the surge would have made swimming impossible anyhow.

"Can you help me? I can't swim, and I am not sure there is another solution," Just Middle Manager called back toward Creator, hoping there was some clever thing that could be done.

"There are many solutions to this problem, really," Creator answered and then continued with a qualifier (Just Middle Manager would soon learn that Creator had a lot of *qualifiers* for most ideas offered). "Regretfully, most of the solutions could not be implemented since the water is rising faster than we have time to execute them. It is too bad, also, because we could do so much here to get you to safety. The most obvious is a bridge or something of suspension which would allow you to simply walk over the danger. Then, perhaps the quickest would be a boat or—"

"A boat! Yes, that is what we need. Do you have a boat?" Just Middle Manager jumped in, hoping to get Creator past the thinking stage and to the application point.

"No, I don't have a boat. Do you have access to one? I could go get it and then navigate it to you," Creator suggested, not really knowing much about boats but thinking that would be a great idea.

"Do I look like I have a boat?" Just Middle Manager yelled.

"You don't have to yell out in such a critical manner. Besides, if the experiment would have worked, you would be praising me right now rather than offering your criticism," Creator said, the voice trailing off. *What really went wrong with the experiment?* Creator thought. *Things looked good in the mind and on paper. But for some reason the explosion was much bigger than needed.*

"What experiment? And what does that have to do with you helping me to safety?" Just Middle Manager called, fearing Creator had become preoccupied with something other than his rescue. Drawing upon lessons learned from Orphan, he did notice that even though the water level was still increasing, the rate of the rise and pace of the flow had diminished significantly.

"Well, if you must know, I was commissioned by Ruler to improve the water flow in and around Celestial City of Influence. But

I fear I used too large of a charge, and the explosion may have damaged the natural damn that protects us from overflow. I am surprised at the amount of the flow. According to my calculations, the flow should decrease before you are fully submerged," Creator yelled, looking up from a pocketsize calculator in time to see that Just Middle Manager was now up to his knees in water.

> Insight: Creator Leaders might often become easily distracted by their own experiments and ideas. Getting lost in these things may cause them to forget the major issue they are facing or to become so overwhelmed that they are frozen by analysis or fatigued by the many thoughts racing in their mind.

"Yes, I think the stream is slowing. But I fear I am still far from safety. How shall I get to the dry land that has provided you refuge?"

"What do you have with you?" Creator called out again, hoping to find some way to help this lone traveler.

"I have very little," Just Middle Manager answered. The water level continued to slow, but the level had reached just below his waist. With the decrease in flow, his panic slowed as well. It helped that he was able to step onto the top of a rock that was protruding up out of the river.

"Certainly, you have more than 'very little,'" Creator called back to him. Having walked along side and now parallel with the refuge rock, Creator was able to talk in more pleasant and lower volume tones with Just Middle Manager.

"By the way, my name is Creator. I am glad to meet you. It certainly would have been a more preferred greeting had you come by a little sooner and avoided this dangerous area."

"I don't believe it was dangerous until someone blew up a dam," Just Middle Manager said, keeping his tone sharp and level loud despite their closer proximity. He purposely didn't offer his name to Creator.

"Again, your voice is overly harsh. I am on the business of Ruler and have full confidence in my ability to get both my project completed and you off that lone rock," Creator said, keeping the pitch much more in line with their nearness and a desire to create a more positive environment.

"I do not mean to be overly critical, but it seems as though your experiment has endangered my life. I think that is cause for some criticism and complaint. Don't you?" Just Middle Manager responded, lowering the pitch of his voice and calming his speech. He too wished to create a good relationship between Creator and himself but only because he thought Creator may be his lone source of rescue.

"You may look at this situation with an untrained eye and see a disaster or, perhaps, even a mess I have created. But I prefer to see the positive side of this," Creator said, looking up and down the river in front of Celestial City of Influence.

"And what would be the positive side of this?" Just Middle Manager asked, fully wanting to be informed or enlightened. "I am Just Middle Manager, and I long for knowledge as I am on a journey to Celestial City of Influence and long to be renamed Next Great Leader. So if you can show me the more positive side of this predicament, it would give me something to think upon as I sit alone helplessly on this rock. This pack on my back can only have its burden lifted by the air of enlightenment."

"Well, first, the positive side of all of this is that Ruler asked me to increase the flow of water around Celestial City of Influence, and I have clearly done that. Second, you are *alone*, but you are not *helpless*. Think beyond your normal way of thinking. Open your eyes. Imagine the many ways you can get off that rock. Or if the only solution is to wait for the flow to subside, visualize what you can do on the rock. No one else has such a chance for this experience. Besides, you said you have 'very little,' but I can plainly see that large pack. Certainly, there is something in there you can use to rescue yourself. Or, perhaps, you could float on the pack itself. What does it contain?"

"It contains both my burden and my discoveries," Just Middle Manager answered, still clinging to the rock but noticing a great improvement in the flow of the water. If he could swim, the river was now moving slow enough for him to do so. But what good are the right circumstances if you don't possess the precise skill sets to make use of it?

"Your burdens *and* your discoveries, how do you mean?" Creator asked, stepping closer to the edge of the water and being drawn by the curious nature of Just Middle Manager's backpack.

"Yes, both burden and discovery are contained within this one package," Just Middle Manager answered as he removed the pack from his back and placed it beside him on the rock. "I left for Celestial City of Influence with a large burden concerning leadership and my particular appetite for it. Along the way, I have met a number of acquaintances that have eased the burden with their wise counsel and even one who carried it awhile for me. Their insights have filled me with great hope that has energized me into thinking I might deserve a change in name to Next Great Leader. But I fear that having come so far, your demolition of the dam may prevent me from entering the gates I can so clearly see."

"It wasn't a demolition," Creator corrected him, feeling as though Just Middle Manager was again on attack. "It was simply a way to divert some additional water into the city's aqueducts, which I am now sure has been accomplished.

"But back to this pack you carry. What advice and counsel have you received? Perhaps there is something within those things that can be made useful for your release? Although, I am not sure of the quality of these new friends you have met on your journey or the value of their words and shrewdness," Creator asked, always wanting to take inventory of the

Insight: Creator Leaders might often view problems in regard to how they can be solved through imaginative ways. This approach may lead them to how a new design might be generated by solving the problem. When looking for answers to problems, the Creator may believe they are personally superior in the development of new solutions and, therefore, discredit others' ideas, not because those ideas lack value, but because the Creator prides himself or herself on those same answers. The Creator may dismiss individuals who they perceive are not as qualified or equipped to develop a solution to the problem(s).

resources on hand that could be used to generate something useful and needful. Creator imagined that by engaging in a discourse with Just Middle Manager, revelation might be gained and that, through that revelation, they would discover the very answers they needed to bring him from his solid but small rock and onto the dry ground. But Creator wasn't sure how much you could trust the counsel and wisdom of those you happened to meet along a lone path. So, at this point, the information in the backpack had little value to Creator.

"The guidance gathered from these trusted souls has been worthy of my trip thus far. If I should sadly be turned away from Celestial City of Influence, my journey will still bear much fruit. If I were to perish on this rock, the knowledge gained will have served me well," Just Middle Manager responded, sounding a little more dramatic than he really wanted. He sat and watched the water inhabit the space just below him. And, in the manner of Innocent, he really did believe that the information gathered had already equipped him more properly, albeit arduously, for leadership.

"You say, 'It has served you well'?" Creator asked. "How has it served you well? If you sit alone on a rock having no solution other than begging for a hand from me for your salvation, how has their input into your pack become of a great service?"

"For one so clever, you have fallen short of even your own scrutiny," Just Middle Manager answered, sensing Creator felt superior to others and much more wittier than most.

"If it were not for the hope provided by Innocent, I would have given up much earlier and

Insight: The Creator may fall into the trap of thinking he or she is much cleverer than they are and, therefore, fail to listen to others or value their input. The Creator can alienate others by their creative life style, not wanting to seem commonplace or ordinary. Because the Creator can become their own worst critic, they may be overly sensitive to the profitability of their own ideas or the ideas of others. This may leave the Creator isolated with their own solutions and/or cause him or her to be overly negative of the solutions of others.

never reached this rock. And Orphan taught me to beware of the dangers of life, enabling me to make it to this very spot. But I fear even Orphan wouldn't have foreseen this dilemma. Furthermore, if it were not for Destroyer, I would still be holding on to that which may have brought me value but never would have moved me on to discover the place I am now."

"Ahh, so you have met with Destroyer?" Creator said, stretching a little taller as if to see beyond to the cliff face and a very familiar log. "I am not so sure the wisdom you gleaned from such a bystander of the road would assist you in your endeavor, for Destroyer is a creature who fails to see the beauty of what can be made out of disaster. I am surprised that the emptiness held by Destroyer has not fully engulfed the soul," Creator went on, making sure if Destroyer were anywhere near the criticism it would not only be heard but possibly felt as well.

"You sound as though you don't fully appreciate Destroyer's philosophies of life. Do you have a way to improve upon what I may have gathered from the lessons learned on that ladder?" Just Middle Manager asked, still looking for a way out of his liquid prison. Regretfully, there was no immediate answer from Creator.

Although only meeting Creator shortly, Just Middle Manager sensed that Creator was preoccupied. Creator seemed to be talking with Just Middle Manager but had a mind full of other projects. *Is one of the possible preoccupations a way to get me off this rock?* Just Middle Manager thought and hoped. *Or has Creator*'s *preoccupation with so many projects and thoughts paralyzed him?*

As Just Middle Manager waited for Creator to respond to the "just-let-go-and-move-on" philosophy of Destroyer, he noticed something rising out of the water. Was something rising out of the river, or were his eyes just longing for any kind of rescue?

"Destroyer's philosophy of life is only half right," Creator spoke.

The sudden firmness and the focus in the voice of Creator caused Just Middle Manager to listen even more intently. Even though he was still a distance from Creator, the water seemed to create a chamber for the sound, enabling them to converse quite easily. Just Middle Manager wondered if Creator knew this, or if it was just a fortunate coincidence of the explosion. Somehow he thought if he asked Creator, there would be talk that this was a natural outcome of the planned experiment.

"Destroyer never leaves that cliff. Letting go is certainly a valuable lesson, but the real beauty in a revolution of life is that you create something new to replace the broken or forgotten. Take this situation you have found yourself in as an example," Creator added, making it sound as though Just Middle Manager had deliberately put himself in this state of affairs.

"The river flowed to one place, and now it flows to another. I have created a new version of something that was sufficient but not excellent. You can't simply destroy; you must also create to complete the circle of a true revolution," Creator said, sitting down on a small rock on the water's edge. Creator's look conveyed that the dialogue they were having was not only complete but over as well.

"But what you created was an accident," Just Middle Manager responded, noticing even more vividly the objects just under the water's surface. It wasn't that something was rising up out of the water; it was that the water was retreating, revealing something to Just Middle Manager.

"You say accident, I say providential," Creator spoke, facial expression clearly portraying a sense of smugness. Creator knew full well that there was no intent in destroying the damn and creating such a large path for the river to flow. Creator also knew with all new design attempts, the unscheduled does not always indicate unwanted or unknown. "If

Insight: The Creator can have such a natural and gifted ability to come up with great and imaginative designs for problems or projects that they can often do so it almost naturally, but often in unconventional ways. What may look like an accident to others is just a natural outcome of the Creator's methods. Others may not see what's in the mind of the Creator, only the finished product. Therefore, they may dismiss the Creator's approach, assuming good accidents happen to us all at one time or another. However, to the Creator the result was actually part of the master plan, or so it seems.

necessity is the mother of all inventions, then *fortunate mistake* is their father."

"Look," Just Middle Manager called out, standing to his feet and pointing down toward the water's surface. "There are some rocks appearing just under the water's face."

"Yes, I see them," Creator responded. "Having opened our eyes and dialogued sufficiently, we have been able to generate a brand-new solution to your difficulty. If you walk slowly and carefully, you should be able to walk across the top of these slightly submerged rocks and find rescue on this shore. Isn't this how it always happens? When you are diligent to wait and to be patient, the new way to do something can suddenly, seemingly just appear."

"I strongly doubt you had much to do with placing these rocks here," Just Middle Manager said as he stepped carefully onto each one. Since the fall from the Destroyer's cliff could still be felt in his leg, he moved slowly but surely to the safety of dry land. To anyone looking out from Celestial City of Influence, it might have appeared as though Just Middle Manager was actually walking on water. But as his feet hit dry ground, the expression on his face showed that he was not supernatural. Only relief could be seen in his visage, not divinity.

"I would not imply that I placed the rocks there," Creator responded. "But I do believe that, if we open our eyes and think beyond our own resources, the answers to problems and the creation of better ways of doing things are right at our feet. And please pardon the pun."

"You are pardoned. And I believe you too have assisted in the easing of my burden and causing the weight of leadership to become lighter to carry," Just Middle Manager said. But with that thought, he suddenly remembered he didn't have his backpack. In his haste to find safety, he had left it silently on his rock of refuge.

"You are probably going to have to walk on water again," Creator said, nodding toward the rock simultaneously as Just Middle Manager had remembered his backpack. This was now the second time that he had left the pack, once on the bed of flowers in Lover's garden and now on this lone rock in the middle of the river. As he walked back across the top of the rocks, it concerned him that he would leave such an important aspect of his journey when faced with personal comfort and now with a crisis of his own safety. What would this teach him about his leadership style and qualifications, he wondered. That thought lingered through his mind as he retrieved the backpack.

He returned to dry land, sat down, and discussed with Creator some of the lessons he had learned along the way. They both thought that the time spent on the rock surrounded by water had been profitable to him. Despite their agreement on that point, Creator still took little responsibility for the predicament Just Middle Manager found himself in. *If Ego is ever present, it is now clinging to Creator,* he thought.

Although they disagreed on the approach, they both approved of the outcome. The flowing of the water through the channels of the city was better, and the lessons learned about completing the circle of a revolution were much needed. Just Middle Manager learned that you can't just put off the old; you have to also put on the new. Letting go, as Destroyer had taught him, was fine. But Creator had shown him that creating something new to take its place was even better.

Although Just Middle Manager felt comfortable with the lessons learned, one thought about Creator caused him to pause. He expressed to Creator that he saw little difference between the Creator world and that of the Seeker life.

"Both of you seem to be on the same mission of discovery and the development of ideas," Just Middle Manager commented. "I shall have trouble keeping the lessons I learned about you separate from those discovered in the dark forest from Seeker."

Creator gave little pause for thought since he had been asked that question countless times from travelers. Turning to Just Middle Manager, he quickly said, "Let me lighten the load of your burden on that thought with some key word choices. When you think of Seeker, I believe you would be thinking of an adventurer. I, on the other hand, would characterize myself as a discoverer. Seeker is more into finding new ideas, while I am energized by new invention. These, I know, are small nuances of our styles but are distinctive."

"Another small difference is that Seeker may be looking for new places, while I am always pursuing new projects. So, you see, there is a difference. One of us is a wanderer to discover new things, and the other is a wonderer about creating new things."

"That does lighten my load somewhat," Just Middle Manager said as he picked the backpack up from the ground and headed toward Celestial City of Influence. Calling back to Creator, he added, "I shall think more about you and Seeker and these small but important differences." In spite of this, as he walked further up the path, he was still cloudy about the two. He could now see there were differences, but he looked forward to understanding them more deeply.

Leaving Creator to future projects, Just Middle Manager walked slowly along the river's edge, enjoying the dry ground beneath his feet. He watched as the water flowed off to his left, and Celestial City of Influence stood strong and secure directly in front of him. The sights and smells of the flowers that lined the city border made it that much more surreal. He was only a short distance from his desired goal. But as he walked up to the city, he thought about what Destroyer had said, *'Just showing up at Celestial City of Influence and expecting to have your name changed to Next Great Leader* is *entitlement.'* That thought began to eat away at his mind. *Is he worthy of Next Great Leader? Would Next Great Leader leave the burden of leadership to seek personal comfort or safety?*

That last reflection began to torture him as he approached the city gates. He wondered if anyone, other than Lover or Creator, saw him leave the burden of leadership for personal reasons.

Pensively he continued up the path to the city, looking one last time back toward Creator, who seemed to already be involved in a new invention of some sort. Just Middle Manager chuckled and walked up to the entrance of the city. Little did he know how serious it was to leave the burden of leadership for one's own personal safety and security. He was about to find out!

Insight Tips for putting *Leader Creator* to work in your own Leadership Style - *Successfully*

1	Embrace the life of entrepreneurship, but realize it is not a normal life. Creators live a different lifestyle and walk to a different sounding drum. Being an entrepreneur is a great life, but because it is not orthodox, it does have its difficulties. You can't have one without the other.
2	Prepare yourself for entrepreneurship by taking risks. Taking a risk is tough, but it is essential for those who wish to be creative. You have to take a risk to make things happen. The Creator will naturally take a risk. For those learning to become Creators, don't be afraid to use training wheels—go slow with it at first.
3	Accept the fact that some things won't work out. If you take a risk, you will ultimately find yourself making more mistakes than others. Don't shy away from taking the risks even if you have multiple mistakes. How does that familiar quote go: *I didn't make a mistake. I simply discovered another way this won't work.*
4	When things work out, don't simply take credit for it because it worked out. Since every failure is not yours, so too not every success is attributed to your genius. Don't try to take credit for something that just happened from your mistake. Be willing to let Fate have her praise.
5	Don't be quick to dismiss the ideas and designs of others simply because they are not your own. Yes, you may have done it differently and even better, in your mind, but others have great ideas and designs as well. Learn to embrace and value what they have and try to blend it with your own rather than reject it because it is not your own. True, real genius is hard to find, but it is possible to have more than one in the room.

Words of Stability and Responsibility from Leader Ruler

"People, people, you are just going to have to form a line and to wait your turn. We must have structure at this gate. You, Desire for Power, get behind Builder of Teams over there. And, you, Struggling with Self, try to keep your focus on the line in front of you." *And good luck becoming any kind of leader much less Next Great Leader,* Ruler thought.

"You all must keep your lines straight and make sure you have the proper documentation. This is for your own good if you hope to enter today. And only use my gate for the proper reason. Remember, there are four gates. If this access gate to Celestial City of Influence is not the right one, remember, there are three other gates to the city. If you need to go to one of the other gates, simply move around the city clockwise to find that gate you want."

Insight: The appetite of a leader following the style of Leader Ruler is about control and structure. Ruler sees life as a system they are responsible for. The Ruler may view others as subjects who will benefit from his or her masterful manipulation of the system for their own good. The Ruler's desire for structure (and control of that structure) motivates their behaviors. Leader Ruler will direct and guide with polices and procedures those they lead, promoting and rewarding those who follow and step in line with their established order. The Ruler sees power as a positive attribute and shares that power with those who equally recognize its value. At the end of the day, the Ruler might say it was a great day because things were put in order and the kingdom is at peace for all the subjects, even if they don't recognize the need for things to be in order.

"Can we go counterclockwise, or will the walls of the city fall in if we do?" a laughing voice was heard from the crowd. The chuckling tone carried a cruel message to Ruler's ears. The vast throng that stood around the gate added to the level of laughter, all at Ruler's expense.

The amusement of the group annoyed Ruler greatly. And, having dealt with it many times in the past, Ruler thought it could be worked through with minor irritation. But Ruler wasn't a jokester. There was a gate for needless humor and sending this irritating pilgrim that way was going to be something that would give Ruler enjoyment.

"Who said that?" Ruler asked, taking control once again. "Which traveler among you hopes to get through my gate bearing credentials of mere jovialness? My gate is for Structured Direction. If you wish to enter into Celestial with humor you need to use Jester's gate: *Irreverent Jubilation.*"

"It was Enjoyment of All. He said it," a voice from the crowd called out as the group had grown to complete silence at Ruler's boorish directives.

Enjoyment of All turned to the traveler to his left and said, "You are properly named, are you not, *Sayer of Much*?"

"Properly named or not, Enjoyment of All, humor is not meant for my gate. If you wish to enter Celestial City of Influence with your brandish wit, you will need to visit Jester's gate. And, for your information, you can go clockwise or counter-clockwise. That is, if you don't get too dizzy going one way over the other," Ruler added, laughing and trying to be comedic in order to show that Rulers have humor as well.

There was no noise from the crowd at first, and then finally Sayer of Much created a forced laugh that others followed. Ruler knew it was a strained gesture, but never the less signaled to Sayer of Much to take a position forward in the line. The rest of the group at this entrance was quick to take note as to how one can move further up the line.

Just Middle Manager watched the entire exchange from a

small distance, having approached Ruler's gate from water's edge. He wasn't sure what he was looking at, but he had learned two things from his observations. The first was he had made the entire journey and knew nothing of "documentation." The second was that Ruler certainly knew what to do to exact influence over a crowd.

> Insight: Because the Ruler is sometimes feared by his or her subjects, they might, at times, offer false praise and sweet talk to get into good standing with Ruler. When this happens, the Ruler may recognize the deceit but still accepts it, feeling as though bogus praise is better than no praise at all.

Just Middle Manager watched in envy as Ruler instructed, directed, and organized the mob. Within moments everyone was either in line or on their way to another gate. Ruler was able to quiet them and guide them with little or no force. Even in the incident with Enjoyment of All, Ruler had showed exactly what it takes to be a leader. That was what Just Middle Manager wanted. That was what he desired and envied.

"You there, traveler, why are you drooling about?" Ruler asked, walking up to Just Middle Manager, who was well into an envious trance, having lost control of most of his senses.

"Drooling? I wasn't aware that I was drooling?" Just Middle Manager replied, awakening as though having been asleep for many nights. He was caught by surprise that Ruler had even noticed him, much less his loss of faculties. He had so much desire for what Ruler demonstrated by way of leadership that he lost total control over his own senses. The envy in his heart had taken control.

"Yes you were drooling. On your journey were you not warned about Envy?" Ruler asked, looking down on Just Middle Manager. Just Middle Manager had stepped into a rather large hole and was knee high in the mud from Celestial's washed out border.

"Yes, I was warned about Envy, but was not instructed much about how to deal with it," Just Middle Manger stated, trying to get out of the hole he had stepped into. Engulfed in Envy, he failed to see the hazard directly in front of him. It was almost impossible to secure a firm grip in the slippery clay forming on the sides of the cavity's walls. And the injury from his previous fall didn't help him with stability. As hard as he tried, on his own he could not manage to get out of this self-made abyss.

"You deal with Envy the same way you deal with Ego," Ruler spoke, the authority of the voice demanding attention from not only Just Middle Manager but the entire group (who stayed in a single file line at the gate's doors not wanting to once again incur Ruler's wrath).

"Ego and Envy are the twin demons of conflict for leaders and followers. Leave no place in your heart for either one. To rid yourself of Envy be content with what you have. Don't be desirous of my ability, as strong and provocative as it may seem for a leader. Seek your own way and use your own gifts. Discover your own appetite for leadership," Ruler said, practically reading the mind of Just Middle Manager.

With those words Just Middle Manager felt humbled that Ruler suggested he may even possess some leadership gifts. But the humiliating thoughts did more than remove the feelings of Envy, they enabled Just Middle Manager to secure help from the other travelers and step out of the small slough of Envy to secure stronger footing.

His humble state allowed him to accept the help of others. *This is a lesson I shall remember,* he thought. Just Middle Manager quickly made a note that humiliation was preferred over Envy. For the former brought help and assistance from others while the latter left you to struggle on your own.

"You are lucky the mire wasn't greater. You did well to control Envy early. Now, who are you and what do you seek at my gate?" Ruler asked, knowing full well who the traveler was.

Just Middle Manager realized this was his moment. He had traveled so far and now found himself in position to ask for a name change. He wished he were not standing in front of Ruler covered in mud, but he knelt down in honor and said his peace.

"Great Ruler, I am Just Middle Manager, and I have traveled

from Follower Village with this large burden on my back to become Next Great Leader. I humbly ask for your permission to enter Celestial City of Influence, so-named," he spoke, head bowed and eyes closed, as though he were making a wish or petition to a superior being.

There was a brief moment of silence and then suddenly a large burst of laughter from both the crowd and Ruler. The jubilation was so loud, Just Middle Manager feared parts of the city wall would be shaken loose. Standing slowly he could hear and see the entire crowd laugh at him. He turned just in time to see Ruler wiping away tears of laughter off his cheek.

Then, more embarrassed than confused, Just Middle Manager asked, "Why do you laugh at my request, Ruler? I have made the appeal with sincerity and good will in my heart. I only wish to be Next Great Leader and to have influence like you over others. You have demonstrated this very thing so marvelously here before me, today."

Ruler was now embarrassed that the laughter could not more quickly be controlled but finally was able to speak, "First, I am flattered that you view me as Great Leader, but I am not, and would not, pretend to be the Royal Eminence. Second, you do not make such a request in this manner. You simply present your documentation at the proper gate, and if it is indeed appropriate, you enter the city. From there, Great Leader is the only one who can designate you Next Great Leader. Only *Great* Leader can put one up for leadership, and only *Great* Leader can bring another down from leadership."

Ruler, as well as the others who had managed to get out of their well-formed line to watch the engaging dialogue with Just Middle Manager, returned to the entrance of Celestial, leaving Just Middle Manager standing alone.

"But, I know not of these gates or of documentation!" Just Middle Manager shouted. "I have not traveled this far, and this long, to be laughed at or to be turned away. I demand instruction and direction from the keeper of this gate!"

The silence that fell over the crowd might have been eerie if it were not for the fact it had a certain serious feel to it. Ruler, obviously taken aback by the tone in Just Middle Manager's voice, turned quickly and walked straight toward him. Having secured better footing after his release from the slough of Envy, Just Middle Manager stood tall and nose-to-nose to Ruler. He was ready to deal with what had to be dealt with. *Warrior would be proud of me,* he thought. *But Orphan would call me a fool for not seeing the danger I was putting myself through.*

"The direction I give you is this," Ruler began, a strong and stern tone couching each word. "There are four gates around Celestial City of Influence. Mine is Structured Direction. If you wish to pass through here, you will need to offer documentation you obtained on your journey that you can demonstrate that you are responsible, directive, structured, and feel comfortable establishing and operating in great systems. If you find yourself capable of these attributes, then proceed to the line and prepare to enter the city. But I sense anyone who leaves his burden of leadership for the purpose of securing personal safety or comfort not only lacks responsibility but also will have difficulty operating in a structured system."

> Insight: Ruler Leaders might often view problems as to how they affect the established rule of law. The Ruler will often view the problem as something that should have been cared for within the system. If there is a problem, the system will either take care of it, or the system will have to be fixed to care for it in the future. When looking for answers to problems, Rulers may, at first, see others as "bucking the system" or even vying for power. When this happens, Rulers may attempt to put the person back in line or dismiss them as having no significance to the overall system.

Ruler had already made a predetermined judgment that Just Middle Manager was not worthy of the gate of Structured Direction, having known he deserted the backpack when he was with Lover and seeing him leave the backpack on the rock as he rushed to safety into the waiting arms of Creator. Up until now, Ruler thought it wise to keep this information private. But with Just Middle Manager's sudden, attacking tone, there was no reason to continue to be confidential. All those at the gate now knew of Just Middle Manager's choices of personal comfort and safety, forsaking the burden of leadership.

"What about the other gates?" Just Middle Manager asked, ignoring the comment about the abandoned backpack. He hoped by ignoring the remark, the others in line, as well as Ruler, would put little stock in the incident. But that wasn't going to happen. The others were already entering into private conversations about Just Middle Manager's selfish acts. He could see the wagging of their heads and knew their conversations were about his misstep. They were all discussing the faults of his leadership.

Ruler, not wanting to further embarrass Just Middle Manager, answered by saying, "The other gates, going clockwise around Celestial, are Hidden Transformation, Superior Information, and Jester's Irreverent Jubilation."

"Actually, I don't think it is Irreverent Jubilation," Sayer of Much interjected. "You have said that twice now. I believe Jester's gate is called Exuberant Jubilation."

"I will call it what I will call it," Ruler responded, turning sharply to address Sayer of Much. The others in line took quick note as to the change in Ruler's demeanor. Sayer of Much simply slid back toward the end of the line, recognizing the disapproving look of Ruler.

Just Middle Manager noticed that Ruler didn't appreciate and showed little value for opposing viewpoints, whether the contrasting opinion was conveyed through humor or expressed for the simple purpose of correcting an obvious error. The jealousy he felt earlier in his heart for Ruler's ability to influence was being replaced by an image of a dictator.

"Ruler, may I have a word with you in private," Just Middle Manager asked. His thinking was that Ruler loved to have others around and would not take criticism well when surrounded by those who might be viewed as royal subjects. *Perhaps that is why Ruler cannot handle criticism,* he thought.

"Of course I can grant you some time, Just Middle Manager,"

Ruler replied, sounding more important than anyone at the gate actually believed. "Why don't we step back toward the water's edge as I have to inspect the work of Creator anyhow?"

"Yes, I was told by Creator it was you who commissioned the increase in water flow. That is the very reason I thought you to be the one."

"You thought me to be the 'one'?" Ruler asked, not following Just Middle Manager's thought.

"The one I should ask for a name change. Since Creator was taking orders from you, I thought you were the one in charge," Just Middle Manager clarified his statement.

"Well, Creator wasn't really taking orders from me. It's just those around Celestial City of Influence rely on me to get things done. I noticed that the aqueducts were severely low and just took upon myself the responsibility to solve the problem. And who better to find a solution than Creator? Besides, Creator is always working some project or invention. We might as well organize all that energy and put it to work within the system, don't you think?" Ruler asked, talking as though everyone would appreciate someone who takes charge when others don't.

Just Middle Manager could see that Ruler really enjoyed a particular way of doing things and that things should be done according to that way. In one respect, he liked that, but also saw the disadvantage of having unmovable procedures.

> Insight: Because the Ruler has such a large commitment for and need to be responsible, they may, at times, take personal responsibility for a problem, even when not asked to do so. They have such a strong desire to improve the system and structure of the organization that they may just take control, assuming that is their job. Others may either feel as though Ruler is overstepping his or her boundaries, or, they may allow Ruler to take action, realizing if the Ruler does, they won't have to.

"You seem to like a good running structure?" Just Middle Manager asked, attempting to clarify rather than confront.

"That I do."

"Do you think all those around you share your enthusiasm and spirit for procedures, policies, and standards of practices?" Just Middle Manager went on to ask, knowing full well there were a lot of people in Follower Village who were not fond of such things.

"No, they don't, regretfully," Ruler answered. "Some like to muddy the system up just so I have to fix it."

"Muddy it up?"

"Yes, they like to find exceptions to the rules or experiences that don't fit the policy. If they just let the system work, then things would be great around here. Take your wandering off the path when you met up with Seeker. If you would have simply left the valley and followed the path, you wouldn't have experienced that nasty fall off the face of the cliff with Destroyer. And you would not have the limp in your walk. If we have a sound plan, we should follow it," Ruler said.

Surprised that Ruler knew so much about him but not wanting to get off subject with the conversation, Just Middle Manager said in response, "But if I wouldn't have followed Seeker's advice, I would not have lightened the load on my back with the insights and teachings of Seeker, Lover, or Destroyer."

"But if you would have followed the path, you would have saved yourself both time and—obviously from the pain in your step—personal injury. What about that pack on your back? Does that contain your documentation to enter Celestial City of Influence?" Ruler asked the questions quickly as he glanced back toward the line behind him. "I must get back to my gate. Can we finish our conversation as I return to assure order is in place?"

Just Middle Manager had to laugh at the very thought of chaos breaking out at Ruler's gate. He knew that so much reverential fear had been established by Ruler's persona that no one would dare attempt to move out of line. And if there wasn't any reverential fear, then there would be enough plain fear to still maintain order. He doubted that Ruler really wanted people to fear, but he also doubted Ruler would make little effort to extinguish the terror if it was helping the system maintain a smooth, running order.

As they walked back toward the city gate, they agreed Ruler's manner would be a good approach for Just Middle Manager to employ as Next Great Leader. In spite of their agreeable nature, Ruler had to disqualify him from entering the gate of Structured Discipline. Just Middle Manager had no real documentation, and Ruler just couldn't look past someone who would go willfully off the path for security, comfort, or both.

Before parting ways, Ruler did give Just Middle Manager a strong piece of advice (at least Ruler thought it was strong and worthwhile advice). "I suggest you go clockwise around Celestial. Your next gate would therefore be Magician's. Since you have no real documentation, Magician would be your best bet to find a way in to Celestial City of Influence."

"Why is that?" Just Middle Manager asked, curious as to who Magician might be.

"Magician's gate is very much different than my gate. I believe that we ought to follow a strict design and plan for things. Magician is much more into transforming and shaping what is there to make it what it might become. You seem to fit that style more than mine. Had you stayed the course of the path and not wandered through the forest, I would have appreciated you entering in at my gate. But the sudden, off-road experiences of your travel did not provide you with proper documentation, and therefore, you need the transforming approach of Magician."

"Don't you think that limits those you allow into the city?" Just Middle Manager asked sharply.

"Yes, I suppose it does. Perhaps that falls into another one of those categories you have been mentioning to my peers along the way?"

"What is that?" Just Middle Manager asked, still curious as to how Ruler knew so much about his journey.

"You have pointed out to a number of us something you call our shadow. I perceive that the shadowy side of my style would be that I always prefer structure and order even when it can't be attained. And I tend to dismiss rather quickly those who don't follow such values."

"Yes, I would agree with that. And I have found much insight from you. It has made my burden lighter. I feel as though I am getting extremely prepared for Celestial City of Influence. Humbly speaking, that is," Just Middle Manager said, looking once again for either Ego or Envy.

"I see that you have a very strong sense of control and order. I am compelled to follow your sense for a strong system. I also feel that I should avoid being too controlling or overbearing. I can see that others look to you to 'take charge' but wonder if that is healthy for you or them. I shall lighten the load on my back with your strengths but not weigh it down any further with the shadowy side of your graces," Just Middle Manager said. He felt comfortable that although he didn't enter the gate, he would take something from it.

After they parted ways, Just Middle Manager could hear Ruler barking more orders. As he went around the corner toward where he was told Magician's gate was located, he could further hear Ruler dismiss someone whose humor had gotten out of hand. *Perhaps,* he thought, *Ruler should also have a small lesson that things don't always have to be so serious to be structured. There should be both humor and efficiency.*

He made a note of that thought and placed it into his backpack. He had plenty of room in the parcel now since so much of his burden was slipping away. He was beginning to replace the heavy questions with lighter answers. The items he had gathered were filling the pack. It now contained some great insights to follow in regard to becoming Next Great Leader. Nevertheless, the pack didn't contain documentation. *Will Magician really help with that,* he thought.

As he turned the corner of the city, surprisingly, one of the most spectacular sights he had seen since he began his trip caused him to stop in his tracks. It was staring right at him, just outside the second city gate. With all the colors that can be imagined, Just Middle Manager was beholding hundreds and hundreds, if not thousands, of butterflies. In the midst of the butterflies was Magician.

How can butterflies and Magician help me with my burden and documentation, Just Middle Manager wondered.

Insight Tips for putting *Leader Ruler* to work in your own Leadership Style - *Successfully*

1	Take charge when you know no one else will. People expect those with the Ruler archetype to take charge. Don't disappoint them. And you don't have to wait until they ask. If you wait until they ask, someone else less prepared or skilled might volunteer, and then you will have the original problem or project to do as well as possibly cleaning up their new mess.
2	Be humble in the exercise of your gifts. Don't leave the servant spirit behind just because you know the situation calls for a *Ruler.* It is okay to lead and rule without being arrogant and condescending. In fact, it is even more productive and appreciated by those you rule.
3	Be careful not to start dictating your wishes and what you know needs to be done. When the Ruler is in the "flow," he or she can become overbearing and bossy. When you find yourself in a stressful situation, you may need to back off and not allow yourself to become too overbearing.
4	Don't be afraid of opposition. Embrace the idea that others may oppose your ideas without actually opposing your leadership. Not every idea or method or policy is right for every situation. So, if others disagree, don't alienate them. Give the same consideration to their ideas, policies, and procedures you want them to give you for your ideas, policies, and procedures. They will appreciate your willingness to hear them and grant you even more power and prestige as a result.
5	Don't look for appreciation or praise just to get the accolades. Because those around you may feel intimidated by you (and they will), you may foster, unwillingly, a false praise from your followers. Make sure you work with them and let them know that you appreciate their loyalty but you must have sincerity. In fact, address that in your system so they know it needs to be done. Show them why and where in the system accolades can be presented.

Words of Transformation and Charisma from Leader Magician

"Step right up ladies and gentlemen. Don't be bashful. Come in here; get closer. That's it. Take a look at this. Never in all your life have you experienced such a wonderful concoction of delightful herbs. To say it has magical powers is to say that the *Mona Lisa* is just a painting. Why, by simply coming into contact with this wonderful elixir, you will discover a marvelous change in both personal behavior and professional outcomes.

"You there, what's your name, and what brings you to my passageway into our fair city?"

"I am Just Middle Manager. I hail from Follower Village, and I desire to enter Celestial City of Influence. Ruler sent me to the gate of Hidden Transformation to the one named *Magician.* Are you the one I search for?" Just Middle Manager spoke, being very careful and watching the crowd diligently. The last thing he wanted to do was to embarrass himself in front of another large crowd, as he had done prior at Ruler's gate.

"Well, yes, I am your humble servant, Magician. But you say you look for a gate called Hidden Transformation?" Magician asked. "Was that the inference or the actual term used by Ruler?"

"Yes, Ruler stated I should attempt your gate, the gate of Hidden Transformation, since I didn't have the documentation for Ruler's gate, called Structured Direction," Just Middle Manager spoke slowly and carefully, still very worried that he was about to embarrass himself in front of this group that had formed a circle around Magician and himself.

Magician's demeanor was so different from Ruler's that he felt a sudden sense of ease, similar to what he felt with Lover. The feeling he had with Magician, conversely, wasn't from a type of bliss or acceptance, as he felt with Lover. This time it was the charm and charisma he could see in Magician. What Ruler may have cultivated in fear from others, Magician produced by magnetism. Just Middle Manager liked Magician right away. Maybe, it was charisma or maybe the confidence that Magician demonstrated. But whatever it was, Just Middle Manager liked it. And whereas Ruler was somewhat stiff and bossy, Magician conveyed that there was something alluring he should follow, as if Magician believed in him.

"First, my dear friend, Just Middle Manager," Magician began speaking, placing an arm around him in a pleasing and accepting manner, "I don't know what you mean by the word *documentation* used by Ruler. I have not heard of that term before you mentioned it here today. And, to correct Ruler, there is nothing *hidden* about my gate. As you can plainly see," Magician stated, moving slightly aside and exposing a very large and wooden gate in the background. Almost on cue, the hundreds of butterflies that had been filling the air around Magician flew up to the gate and attached themselves to it as a cloak would to a cold and weary traveler.

Continuing, Magician said, "I think Ruler's desire for order, structure, and design may have once again caused an innocent but potential leader to conclude the wrong assumptions as to entrance into Celestial."

"And, yes, there is transformation at this gate, but nothing is hidden except to the one who wishes not to see. I fear my dear friend, Ruler, can only see what Ruler's system contains. But outside that system, there are many who can qualify for leadership and entrance to the Great City of Influence if they but succumb to even a minor transformation of themselves."

"For instance, Just Middle Manager, you should note that one small but purposeful sip of my inexpensive Exchange Elixir will transport you from what you are to what you need to become.

Perhaps the only documentation needed is a simple *transformation of self*."

With all the dialogue, Magician never took the brightly enrobed arm off Just Middle Manager's shoulders. As though they were best friends for life, Magician's touch seemed to work in partnership with the small bottle being hawked.

Insight: The appetite of a leader following the style of Leader Magician is about transforming the world around them. Magician sees potential in all and how everyone can be transformed. The Magician may view others as potential targets of change, even if they can't see that potential within themselves. The Magician's desire to bring that transformation about through a variety of methods motivates their behaviors. Leader Magician will inspire those they lead to see what can become of people, organizations, projects, or circumstances, promoting and rewarding those who gather around to support his or her cause and desires. At the end of the day, the Magician might say it was a great day because they were able to change someone or something, even if it didn't want to be changed, using their magical powers to lead, guide, inspire, or positively manipulate their subjects into becoming what he or she believes these subjects should become.

As Just Middle Manager looked at the little container, he could make out a small logo affixed to Magician's secret potion. Wrapped across the bottle in what appeared to be a hand-painted design was a picture of a butterfly. And, as though the creature had a hand, a small magician's wand was protruding from under its wing. On the end of the wand, for special effect, were small lines protruding from the baton to demonstrate the *poof* effect of a magician's charm.

"I perceive, Magician, that you believe I lack some quality of leadership and need a personal transformation. A 'poof' may be the phrase in your world," Just Middle Manager said, his voice sounding suspicious but also disapproving of the thought.

"I only perceive you are looking for something you yourself say you do not have. And along your journey, you have solicited the assistance from others in obtaining it," Magician responded, releasing the shoulder of Just Middle Manager for the first time in a manner similar to an angler who would release back to the water a netted fish that still needed growth.

"If you desire this 'documentation' Ruler spoke of, then I offer you the opportunity to gain it," Magician said, the intensity of his charm and magnetism increasing with each word.

"What do you perceive I need to change, Magician?" Just Middle Manager asked, hoping to gain insight. (Magician's allure seemed to once again be working on him.)

"It is not for me to say. You have come here looking for something, for I perceive the pack on your back was at one time awkwardly laborious and even now you seem to struggle with it," Magician said, all the while receiving payment for two small bottles of elixir from another weary traveler named Gullible.

"Yes, this load has been heavy at times. But it has been lightened by the many I have met along the way. I perceive, perhaps, you can also provide me with some insight to lessen its sting," Just Middle Manager stated, while adding, "If you would be so inclined?" Taking the pack off his shoulders and laying it on the ground, he was careful not to put it somewhere he might later come to forget about it. Ruler's lesson had been learned.

"I think it best that I modify my methods and judgments about you, Just Middle Manager. I shall adapt the way we approach your situation. I prefer to work with you as a

Insight: Magician Leaders might often view problems as to what can transpire as a result of them. They may be actually titillated by problems. The bigger the problem, the more excitement generated. The Magician will often view the problem as a chance to use some magic powers they believe they possess. When looking for answers to problems, the Magician will adapt and adjust their own personal methods and style to meet the demands of the problem presented. This flexibility allows them to work with a variety of situations, since they are not locked in to a single system. The Magician doesn't believe in cookie cutter answers and will strive to invent ("poof") a new way to handle the problem. The Magician also may be drawn to the crowd. For any good Magician needs two things: a good trick and an audience to see the trick performed.

fellow partner. As though we were a team," Magician said, once again putting a soft hand on Just Middle Manager's shoulder.

"I see that you are a learning soul and worthy of what I may offer. Come let us step over into the shade of this tree and converse about how I might be able to assist you. But let's not get too far from those who may want to purchase some of my wares, and those who may be watching may actually benefit from my ability to work with and to solve your current dilemma."

Magician must have signaled to the hoards of butterflies fluttering about; for as they stepped underneath the leafy boughs, the creatures landed above them as if creating an umbrella of both shade and ambiance.

"Isn't that interesting that the butterflies followed us to this shelter, Just Middle Manager?" Magician stated, looking up into the limbs of the tree just as the butterflies took their sanctuary. Continuing, Magician added, "Perhaps, they believe we are on the right course."

> Insight: Leaders with Magician tendencies may see coincidence of circumstances as a sign of good fortune or approval of approach. Because these "lining of the stars" can feel so strong at times, Magicians may come to the point of relying upon these mere coincidences rather than simply noticing their existence. The coincidence may then become their new technique rather than a past guide.

"You did not signal to them to do that?" Just Middle Manager asked, joining Magician gazing up toward the beautiful creatures perched above.

"Of course I did not signal to them. You must believe I have some great power if you believe I can command even a small butterfly to do my bidding?" Magician exclaimed, the humbleness of attitude not sounding as genuine as hoped.

"I do not believe you have any powers, Magician, much less great power," Just Middle Manager answered. "I do believe you are very capable, obviously, and have the ability to teach me something about leadership. But I will not drink your potion without understanding why I should and what it contains!"

"I perceive your attitude is the result of meeting my friend, Orphan?" Magician responded, wanting to set Just Middle Manager at ease and perhaps regain the charm lost with the earlier poor attempt at humility.

"Do you know Orphan?" Just Middle Manager asked, opening himself up and falling into Magician's allure.

"We have passed a time or two," Magician answered, not really remembering or caring if the two of them had actually spoken. "I only mention the name because you are practicing so well the arts learned from such an astute teacher."

Insight: Magician will often use the connections he or she has (whether real or made up), as a way to show the extent of their secret powers. The Magician may even enjoy name-dropping as a way to assure a would-be client or audience member that they are credible and have something to offer. Like posters about the big attraction, Magician uses names and associations to publicize the show.

Just Middle Manager enjoyed the compliment from Magician. And, whether genuine or said fallaciously, it once again set him at ease with Magician.

"I perceive you have a false impression of me, my dear friend," Magician stated as they sat together under the colorful canopy. "Perhaps we need to take a moment for me to reassure you that I am very much concerned for your welfare and that burden you carry so closely. For I perceive it may be coupled to your back, but it is very much worn on your heart."

"Yes, it is a terrible burden I bear fully to my soul. I truly desire to be Next Great Leader and no longer Just Middle Manager. But I perceive I have no documentation to prove my worth. I fear I have traveled this long and winding path only to come short of both goal and desire," Just Middle Manager stated, lowering his head and looking down at the pack still securely settled at his feet.

"I fear you have lost some of that hope and vision you first entertained with Innocent, my dear Just Middle Manager," Magician said, fully knowing that if someone had come that far along the path to Celestial City of Influence they would have had to come across Innocent at one point or another. And, quickly continuing before Just Middle Manager could question any actual encounter about Innocent and thereby test Magician's creditability, Magician said, "I perceive we need to take a moment for you to relax and reflect about your journey so far and, perhaps, gather some much needed confidence and comfort concerning the value of both your trip and your nature. Why don't you simply close your eyes and think through your past accomplishments along this long but important journey. Meditation might be more beneficial right now than any words. For mere words may have to submit for a moment to the way of spirit."

With a hand firmly on Just Middle Manager's shoulder, Magician's eyes closed, launching what appeared to be a quiet sense of meditation and reflection. The crowd that had gathered around them simply looked at each other and began to slowly bow their heads and close their eyes as well. But most looked as though they had never practiced the art of soulful contemplation, and their level of discomfort showed plainly.

Insight: The Magician Leader is well aware of the physical, spiritual, and the unconscious world. It is part of the allure of their magic when working with others, to call upon these various aspects of life, using them to their full advantage in the healing, transforming, and/or conversion process. There may be no aspect of the metaphysical world or the world of science that is out of bounds as a possible skill set for their powers. Like a potpourri of fragrance, they all can be used to bring about change.

Just Middle Manager wasn't sure what to do any more than the crowd did. He did notice one soul, Strong Doubter, quietly slipping away from the crowd and heading back toward Ruler's gate. But after a few moments, Just Middle Manager also closed his eyes and began to reflect on the many friends he had met along the way. It wasn't long before he was actually reliving each spot on his journey where each companion had touched his life. He wasn't actually conscious of it, but a smile was showing across his face as he remembered Warrior poking a sword into the bushes searching the shadows for the evilness of Ego and Envy. The smile grew even larger as he deliberated on the look of Destroyer's face while standing over him after his fall from the rock face, the pain in his leg smilingly gone from memory for the moment.

After some time, Magician spoke, awakening Just Middle Manager from his trance-like state. "You seem to be in a better spot already."

He didn't know how long he had been meditating, but when Just Middle Manager made his return to the consciousness of the living, he could see that most of the crowd had dispersed; and it was only he, Magician, and a few remaining stragglers still seated under the shade of the tree and the awning of butterflies.

"Wow! That felt good just to remember where I have been so far on my journey," Just Middle Manager said, looking toward Magician for really the first time. He continued, smiling gently at Magician, "I do not believe you have any actual secret powers, but I would say you have given me some great guidance. Taking the time to reflect allowed me to leave the overwhelming state I found myself in; recalling some great memories and remembering some of the great truths from along the way. It has left me very much in an altered state."

"I never said I had any powers. I am often misunderstood in this way. I simply believe that most of us have a capacity within us for many things, and we only need to tap into those resources to discover our own power and the magic of self-transformation," Magician responded, knowing full well that when misunderstood any real healing powers are severely diminished.

"Perhaps many believe your charisma overshadows your true skills. Maybe they believe the charm you use to reach them actually diminishes your insights into the subconsciousness of their world. Others may believe you lack substance, and you try to disguise that shortcoming with potions and charms," Just Middle Manager stated.

"That is often the case. Some view me mistakenly, as though I am or desire to be, a special spiritual guide with mystical powers and practices. But, I am like all others. I simply believe in the power of someone who desires to change and transform themselves. Especially if they have the right tools, support, and counsel," Magician responded, looking at the few lone travelers who had remained.

Speaking to Just Middle Manager but looking toward the small, lingering crowd, Magician continued, "If those who wish transformation will but combine their inner values with their outward behaviors, they will see tremendous changes. They can become more than they could ever wish to become. They just have to make the effort to get fully inside themselves. The combination and transformation of their conscious and subconscious values and behaviors can become something beautiful and rewarding for both themselves and for the benefit of others."

"Like an ugly worm that spins a cocoon around itself and eventually comes forth as a beautiful butterfly, offering enjoyment and pleasure to those who see it," Just Middle Manager added, thinking he had discovered a new truth to replace the old and tired question of leadership still remaining in his pack.

"Yes, that is it. It is not about what I may provide in a secret potion. It is entirely the ability of those who wish transformation to look within. I only humbly supply the guidance and support where needed."

"So are the butterflies simply here on their own, or do you manipulate them as a way to sell your vision and formulas for life?" Just Middle Manager asked, hoping to discern more properly between Magician's strengths and shadows.

"The butterflies are a symbol of what takes place at my gate. Whereas Ruler would refer to it as the Gate of Hidden Transformation, I prefer to call it the Gate of Second Chance: All who enter Celestial City of Influence from my gate need only the documentation of a transformed life. They simply need to see the potential of the human spirit and that everyone can become great leaders if they wish to alter their being on the altar of self-transformation. My secret potion is nothing more than the impetus, pushing others to look within."

"It is only after we discover what is within that we can truly hope to conform to what is outside. Ruler is marvelous at securing conformity to lines, procedures, and customs. Mindless drones follow Ruler's prescribed methods and manners. Still, without the Magician's life of transformation on the inside first—a magical *poof* of heart and soul—there is only outward conformity. I would not suggest to any traveler neglecting Ruler's life in the cocoon. I only want them to go through a transformation while they are there. The cocoon protects the transformation. The transformation gives the cocoon meaning. For if it were not for the transformation to the butterfly, the cocoon is simply a soft, but deadly coffin."

"But don't you fear that when others drink the cool refreshment of your words they will also want to simply follow *your* patterns for life and not really investigate their own inner self or specific needs?" Just Middle Manager asked as he looked to his right and noticed Gullible chugging both bottles of the elixir he previously purchased.

Insight: The danger of Magician's charm can be seen in the countless followers who drink unwittingly from Magician's Kool-aide, simply because they are captivated by salesmanship or a creative sales pitch. The Magician must be careful not to use his/her well-oiled words to cause others to act in a way they are not yet capable of acting.

Out of the corner of the eye, Magician also caught a glimpse of Gullible but quickly turned to sell the feeble elixir to newcomers who had now gathered at the sight of the butterflies hovering above. It was as though Magician made a conscious effort to ignore Just Middle Manager's question.

As he walked away from the Gate of Second Chance, Just Middle Manager realized it wasn't a conscious effort to ignore his question that caused Magician to return to pitching the potion. It was the very fact that the shadowy side of Magician's style, like the shadowy side of those he had met, was very much below the subconscious. The very art Magician portrayed in strength, again like the others, was indeed the weakness. For if Magician was all that skilled at harmonizing all the aspects of the known and the unknown (the seen and the unseen), then one would think there would be enough skill to see one's own shortcomings. But like the others Just Middle Manager had met, the shadowy side of Magician's style was firmly veiled by its very strengths.

Just Middle Manager knew he had learned one very important truth from Magician: The only 'documentation' he needed was simply his ability to allow those things he had learned in his life and along this journey to harmonize and thus transform him. He wasn't yet knowledgeable as to what he would become, but he could feel he was like a worm in a cocoon, transforming into something. And he knew he liked the feelings of the conversion. *What color will I be when the metamorphosis is complete,* he wondered.

That thought seemed to seep deeper into Just Middle Manager's mind as he made his way clockwise (he didn't want to upset Ruler) around Celestial City of Influence. As he looked behind him, he could hear the faint but familiar words of Magician calling out to other travelers. "Step right up ladies and gentlemen. Don't be bashful. Come in here; get closer. That's it. Take a look at this. Never in all your life have you experienced such a wonderful concoction of delightful herbs. To say it has magical powers is to say that the *Mona Lisa* is just a painting ..."

Just Middle Manager realized that was just Magician's shtick; nevertheless, it seemed appealing. *Maybe I should get a shtick,* he thought. But he neither knew what the shtick would be nor how to sell it. Magician sounded so smooth when speaking the magician lingo. Just Middle Manager feared he would sound unrehearsed and childish. *But what's wrong with being childish,* he thought. *I don't have to pretend to know everything. This is, after all, a learning process!*

The journey was a learning process, but as he made his way around the third corner of the city wall, he realized his thought might be inappropriate at least for this, the third gate to the city, for this entrance had presence. Ruler's entrance to the city was nondescript, and Just Middle Manager couldn't really see Magician's gate for all the butterflies. But the entryway in front of him was majestic at first sight, reminding Just Middle Manager of a large state house or government building. The four ivory pillars acted like sentries, standing tall and erect as if protecting some treasured cache. Just Middle Manager would soon learn the focus of their vigilant gaze.

	Insight Tips for putting *Leader Magician* to work in your own Leadership Style - *Successfully*
1	Don't rely on your charisma more than your content. It is very easy for Magician to rely upon his or her charming exterior in life and not develop real inner concrete content. Those who rely upon charm will and can subdue a variety of people. But, effects of that persuasion are short lived as compared to the preferred long-lasting consequences.
2	Don't allow your charisma to overpower your content. It is one thing to allow your charm and great people skills to replace your content, but it is another to allow them to overpower the meaningful and solid words of counsel and advice you offer. When this happens, others will mistake the charisma for content and leave having had a good conversation but not being fully transformed or converted.
3	Remember, not everyone needs a transformation. Simply because you see potential in others doesn't mean they see potential. Or, worse, just because you see potential doesn't mean others see the same potential for themselves. They may see something quite different or desire something different. You shouldn't always look at people for the purpose of converting them. You can lose some good friends and family who don't want to experience the magician's *poof.*
4	Alert others to the power and pleasure of your Kool-aide drink. Others may just drink away because your words are so cool and pleasurable. It is your responsibility to introduce to them their responsibility to filter and qualify your message. Invite them to criticize and question your message before they drink at the cistern of your well.
5	Don't drink only your own Kool-aide. Investigate and learn from others. Remember everything that is coincidental isn't always a statement of validity. Search out new thoughts and new ways to look at things. Don't get caught following the same shtick just because it is familiar and you have customers willing to listen. Their applause doesn't mean the trick was good. It just may mean they haven't seen it before. So, don't be afraid to question your material and work on some new tricks now and then.

Words of Truth and Wisdom from Leader Sage

As Just Middle Manager stood—enthralled by the vastness of the city gate before him—he determined that it must be the main entrance to Celestial City of Influence. Having climbed the numerous marble steps before him, he circled one of the four mammoth pillars. He stood next to the pure white column and rubbed his hand across the embossed etching on a plaque attached across what appeared to be the face of the post. Just Middle Manager noticed there were several plates on each of the four supports. He drew himself closer to read the one directly in front of him; it was attached to the second column from the right and read:

> To all who enter this hallowed place: May the knowledge and wisdom you acquire from this site guide you and protect you from the deceptions of this world. May you find truth here. But if you cannot find truth, then may you find the skill sets and skepticism you need to find truth later down the path you tread. And may the burden of your heart be set free by the truth learned from this juncture. For paths that do not lead through this intersection of truth can only leave your burden heavy and soul wanting. And having spent time in this place, may you satisfy the itching in your minds for pure knowledge and deep truth.

As Just Middle Manager read through the inscription, he was struck by its inference. *What if I had missed this place*, he asked himself. Frightened by that thought, he began to circle around each of the four pillars, further drinking in the captions and writings secured to each. Most had similar messages to the first one he read, but some of the others were also affixed with copies of certificates of merit or diplomas of accomplishments.

One tablet, because of its size, caught his eye in particular, but it was attached well above his line of vision. As he stretched high enough to gaze and contemplate its thought, his foot slipped from the top step, and he quickly fell back toward another traveler proceeding along the steps below.

"I am so sorry, dear friend," Just Middle Manager stated, nearly knocking the traveler down. To be courteous, Just Middle Manager knelt to pick up a parchment he had clearly dislodged from the traveler's hand during the collision.

"That is entirely alright," the traveler said calmly. Nevertheless, he quickly reached up and snatched the rolled paper from Just Middle Manager's hand.

In an apologetic tone, Just Middle Manager offered a handshake and said, "I was trying to read what was inscribed at one of the higher points of this column and lost my balance. Are you okay? I am Just Middle Manager."

"Yes, I am fine. My name is Learner of Much, and if you are enchanted by these writings, wait until you actually talk to Sage," Learner of Much responded, ignoring the handshake and choosing rather to point toward someone standing near the fourth and final column. It appeared as though the figure was stationed there alone, as though meditating.

"Sage, you say?" Just Middle Manager asked, looking past Learner of Much to study the body before him. Although the long white robe he saw looked similar to the one Lover was wearing, Just Middle Manager noticed the one worn by Sage was much more formal and showed some sense of rank. A long white sash around the neck of Sage seemed to extend down the face of the robe, blending in so well it made it difficult to differentiate between robe and sash. Just Middle Manager thought he was looking at a miniature replica of a god.

"Yes, it is Sage. Why read the writings when you can talk to the one who composed them?" Learner of Much said. With a sense of urgency across his face and his hand firmly clinched to the manuscript, he continued his descent down the stone steps, rushing toward the fourth corner and final gate of Celestial City of Influence.

"Wait, dear friend, what is that you clutch in your hand?" Just Middle Manager asked, taking his eye off Sage, following Learner of Much down the stone steps, calling after him, but failing to catch either his ear or his eyes.

Insight: The appetite of a leader following the style of Leader Sage is about seeking truth and converting it to deliverable wisdom for others. Sage sees the patterns in common knowledge. The Sage may view others as either potential sources for knowledge or students to be taught his or her wisdom. The Sage's desire to learn new things or to relay that learning to others motivates their behaviors. Leader Sage will inspire those they lead to seek truth and the power found in it, promoting and rewarding those who expand their pool of knowledge and seek a better understanding of the world around them. At the end of the day, the Sage might say it was a great day because they were able to both learn something new and deliver that knowledge to a lesser soul, enlightening them to the greater truth they may have missed along the way but are now being provided for the betterment of their soul.

"He holds in his hand his rite of passage into Celestial City of Influence," Sage said, appearing behind Just Middle Manager but clearly remaining further up the marble staircase.

As Just Middle Manager turned, he could see Sage standing well above him. The white sash and long robe offered even more mystique when Just Middle Manager could see the long silver hair flowing from Sage's head and draping the shoulders like vines of luscious grapes. Although the city wall was entirely blocking the sun, he thought he could make out a glow of light surrounding Sage's head from behind. Later, he would come to believe his imagination was simply playing tricks on him.

Sage stared at Just Middle Manager for a brief moment and then said, "How are you today, traveler? What wisdom do you bring me from your journey?"

"Well, I'm feeling great. But what do you mean, 'What wisdom do I bring'?" Just Middle Manager asked, really not sure what *wisdom* his journey had actually provided him. He knew he had learned some valuable lessons because the pack on his back that began with such heavy questions was now lighter with answers. Just Middle Manager would prefer to characterize these lessons as practical truths. But was the truth he learned from his recent friends the wisdom Sage now requested?

"Yes. You have been on a very long journey, have you not? And, as with every sojourn, there should certainly be wisdom gained from it, don't you think?" Sage asked, slowly descending the marble steps one at a time. The pace of the descent seemed to match the aura about Sage. There was a sense of calmness and control in the decline like someone who was not about to be rushed or bothered by the little things of life. It was like someone who had obtained great honor was now lowering to speak to another of lesser order.

Insight: The Sage, because of their deep desire for thought and analysis, can be seen as calm in most situations others are not. Their calmness can appear as being detached and uninvolved, but it is actually their ability to analyze and deduct unemotionally. As a result, they are seldom bothered by the trivial and may seem aloof at times.

"One of the wisest men of all ages, Solomon, tells us to 'number our days so that we may gain a heart of wisdom,'" Sage added, quoting a proverb from the noted ninth-century Jewish leader. "I would think if you took account of your journey, there would be enough to

Insight: The Sage is a well-read and knowledgeable leader who prides himself or herself in knowing the ancient or latest theories, thoughts, and philosophies of life. It is not unusual for a leader of Sage quality to quote a variety of authors in any one discourse, some even of opposing beliefs. This can be done to augment the conversation or to simply posture and to impress the listeners.

harvest for us both to partake and thus grow and gain in knowledge and wisdom."

Since Just Middle Manager was not well-read, he decided it best not to challenge Sage in regard to any quote, but he did find it enticing to discuss further what he may or may not have learned from his journey. But not feeling comfortable standing lower than Sage as he spoke, he took a couple of steps up the marble walkway and said, "I am not sure that what I discovered along my journey would be termed by a person of your high degree as 'wisdom.' But as a result of this experience, I do think my load is lighter, and I am much more equipped to be renamed Next Great Leader, should I be allowed to enter Celestial City of Influence."

Ignoring the comment about being allowed to enter Celestial, Sage spoke, in almost a commanding fashion, "Rehearse for me your travels, and allow me to interpret what may be learned."

Just Middle Manager wanted to question why the review of his journey in the ears of Sage would be necessary, and why Sage had to "interpret" anything. But he thought it best not to direct the conversation in that direction at this time. He would, mistakenly, keep the thought active in his mind for some time.

Sage, as though reading the thoughts of Just Middle Manager, took one more step toward the top, remaining higher

---

Insight: Sage Leaders might often view problems through analytical glasses. They enjoy putting difficulties under the microscope of their knowledge, wisdom, and paradigms. The more complex the problem, the more excited they get (as a result they can have a disdain for the mundane and normal). The Sage will often view the problem as a chance to challenge and expound their knowledge and philosophy. When looking for answers to problems, the Sage may discover patterns and issues others may miss, which only adds to both their excitement and feelings of superiority. The Sage may look with such scrutiny at a problem that they may see difficulties arising in the analysis of other's deductions and become overly critical of their analysis. This may, at times, make them appear to be picky or too exact in scrutiny. However, this ability to look deep into issues makes them excellent problem solvers. They often are willing to look beyond even their own prejudice to solve a specific issue.

---

than Just Middle Manager, and said, "I only ask in order to provide my analysis of your journey. I enjoy the deduction of truth and the discovery of patterns others may have missed."

"Do you believe I may have overlooked something along my journey? Because I assure you that I didn't," Just Middle Manager stated, sounding threatened by Sage's remark. "The lightness of my pack is evidence that I have replaced the heavy questions, noticeably present at the beginning of my journey, with the lighter answers of truth learned along the way."

"Come with me. I'll explain. Please have a seat, while I enlighten you as to the meaning of my words," Sage said, walking toward a large desk Just Middle Manager hadn't even noticed before. It was well-hidden behind the four large white pillars. Bulky and made of wood, it was covered with books, notes, and parchment paper. The chair that Sage sat in was behind the desk and was very large. Even though Sage was of greater height and weight than most, the chair had a swallowing affect.

"I believe we must meticulously look into the possible lessons learned along your journey," Sage said, retrieving and lighting a pipe at the same time.

The opposite chair, the smaller one, and the one motioned by Sage that Just Middle Manager should occupy, was overtly smaller than the other chair and the desk itself. As he took his seat in this chair, Just Middle Manager felt like a small child at a large dinner table.

"Let's begin by you telling me where you think you are in your journey," Sage stated, puffing repeatedly on the pipe and igniting the burn. Its aroma only supplemented the moment for Just Middle Manager. The smell of the pipe, the overly large desk, and the feelings of being much less than Sage made him feel as though he was sitting down to discuss a recent paper with a university professor, a paper he may have written only to fail an assignment.

"Well, up until I met you, I felt as though something was transforming within me. I was excited about the transformation. I can feel something taking place within me," Just Middle Manager answered, remembering the feelings he had when he left Magician and the butterfly moment in his stomach.

"'Feelings,' my dear traveler, are not typically a reliable source for deductive reasoning," Sage stated, absent from any emotion. "I would suggest that we simply, as I stated before, rehearse your travels. Perhaps the nuggets of knowledge are just simply below the surface."

Just Middle Manager was taken aback by Sage's impression that he hadn't already gathered "nuggets" of truth and that his feelings were inappropriate or not worthy to determine what was happening on his journey. But nevertheless, this expedition had taught him to cherish any new acquaintance and to not dismiss another until he heard them out. *Maybe that is a practical truth I should put into my bag,* he thought.

Insight: Because Sage relies so much upon critical analysis and factual evidence, he or she can dismiss emotions and feelings as unvalued and unreliable commodities in the commission of sound reasoning. Yet, the Sage's own personal intuition can be a great source for reasoning and decision-making.

"I would be glad to rehearse my journey with you, Sage. But, I fear you may have already dismissed my *own* gleanings that I have already placed in my backpack. Nevertheless, do you want me to share with you the mere events of my travels or the insights I gained from them?" Just Middle Manager asked, trying to hide his frustration with Sage. He did simultaneously feel a small, evil twinge in his heart. Ego was rising slowly and he could feel it.

"I assure you I haven't discharged your findings, Just Middle Manager," Sage responded, using his name for the first time. "I only wish to learn from your travels and thus enlarge my own reservoir of truth."

Just Middle Manager felt bad that he had so judged Sage. That feeling caused him to slump even further down in his chair. But rather than give in to his feelings, he highlighted for Sage, step-by-step, the various events of his journey and the tutors he had met along his way.

For some reason when he used the word *tutor,* there was much discussion between them as to what he may have meant. It was decided, although the word tutor would not be an inappropriate term to use, the word *coach* might be better. They both agreed these figures in Just Middle Manager's journey had indeed coached him through some event in which he was able to gain a stronger grip on the meaning and measure of his own leadership style.

"So I believe each of these coaches has given me some clear lessons to use as a leader," Just Middle Manager finished.

"But do you fully understand the connection between those you have met?" Sage asked, as though there was some hidden meaning which had escaped Just Middle Manager.

"What connection are you referring to?" he asked, developing a more favorable demeanor toward his new teacher. He also wanted to at least sound receptive to a possible learning moment.

"As an example, let's take the dichotomy between Innocent and Orphan," Sage began, leaning into the large desk and toward the diminutive Just Middle Manager. With a tone of voice that now matched the professor motif, Sage continued as if addressing a classroom of freshmen students, "Innocent may have given you the attitude of hope and anticipation, but Orphan tempered this lesson with insight about the dangers and perils of life. Living a life of the Innocent without the balance of the Orphan would be dangerous and immature. Conversely living a life of the Orphan without the symmetry of Innocent would be extremely dark and pessimistic. Together, they give us a great sense of shrewdness. Do you see?"

"Yes, I do, and although I had similar thoughts along the way, I wouldn't have been able to actually articulate them at this depth," Just Middle Manager stated, trying to sit higher in his chair. He felt like a child on a small stool and wanted to change the look. Despite his efforts, as hard as he tried, he still sat much lower than Sage's desk, looking more like a mere youth than the fully grown man he was. *Was this really happening, or was this what it is like to be in the presence of a real Sage,* he thought.

"Tell me; are there other combinations within these coaches

of mine?" he asked, hoping his demeanor would give him some value in the presence of Sage if his posture did not. He was also hoping to answer some of the final questions in his backpack about leadership and the style he should invoke should he ever get the chance to be Next Great Leader.

"Yes, take the other two you came across in the valley, Warrior and Caregiver. The former taught you there are rewards necessary to fight for and discipline will enable you to obtain them. But it was Caregiver's lesson from the rut which taught you that to fight and to war with no sense of care and concern would be cruel and ineffective. Warring for warring's sake is callous, but also, caring for caring's sake can foster weakness and a sense of entitlement in others. Together, they teach us a proper balance of accountability and a sense of duty, something a leader must possess as he or she enters Celestial City of Influence."

With this last statement, Just Middle Manager's heart jumped. Sage had actually said something to him about the entry to Celestial. He was excited at the prospects of finally knowing what he had to have, become, or know. Ruler seemed to want him to have something, while Magician wanted him to become something. But it was Sage who seemed to want him to know something. *What is it*?

"Tell me then about the four I met in the forest area near the river?" Just Middle Manager asked, feeling as though he was once again filling his backpack with the pleasant air of truth.

"I would hope you could see their connection, yourself," Sage stated, making Just Middle Manager feel once again undeserving of entry into Celestial City of Influence. Sage, noticing how the statement landed upon Just Middle Manager's heart, quickly continued, "But, these are not easy lessons. Only the most astute travelers actually see them."

"If you noticed, the lesson of Seeker was to go out and explore and to discover new and risky things beyond the normal path of life. But by doing so, you leave the well-worn path in hopes that you will see grander sites. You should have been able to see that living the life of Seeker without the equilibrium of Lover would be a life of loneliness and alienation. One cannot always go about the forest seeking new things without also experiencing a life of living alone. But Lover taught you to embrace and to value the ever-present bliss of the moment you are in and those who are in it with you. But if you get lost in the ecstasy of the moment and hold to it too tightly, you may only live with memories and objects of the past. You may also hinder others from ever experiencing their own bliss, fencing them in and constraining them for your own benefit. But when the dichotomy of Seeker and Lover are in harmonious balance, you are able to discover a true identity and sense of vision. With the one, you are seeking the new, and with the other, you are embracing the old."

"Leaving the forest area, we turn to Destroyer and Creator. I hear, by the way, you came over the rock face with a real thud," Sage continued, showing some humorous emotion for the first time in their discussion. But, as though he had revealed a side of himself he would rather surpass, he continued soberly, "Destroyer was teaching you to let go of things, especially when they lose value, purpose, or real need. But if you live a life only of the Destroyer, you will soon be empty since you will always be letting go but creating nothing new. So before you could fully leave the protection of the forest, you had to learn to create. This allowed you to pass over the river. Creator is a valued coach in the life of the traveler. But as you could see, Creator can become so overwhelmed with too many inventions and projects that dangerous mistakes can be made. Creator, in full mode and unchecked, can lack focus and decisiveness. If Creator could ever get along with Destroyer and Destroyer with Creator, you would see a wonderful revolution take place. The art of letting go at the appropriate time is not only based upon the insignificance of the thing you are letting go, but also in the beauty of the thing you have created to take its place."

"I am beginning to see some things I did miss along the way," Just Middle Manager humbly confessed, feeling the presence of Ego slipping back into its dark shadows and away from his heart and attitude.

"But we haven't completed the journey, have we? You did meet two other coaches here at the city walls, did you not?" Sage said, now in full-teaching mode.

Just Middle Manager could tell that Sage was enjoying the delivery of truth and wisdom. It was as though learning was a good part of life for Sage and brought energy and excitement. But the delivery of truth and insight brought even more enthusiasm to the Sage life.

"Yes, besides you, I have met with Ruler (a somewhat bossy coach) and with Magician, who gave me my feelings of transformation and change I spoke to you about a moment ago. I see now how foolish I was to simply rely upon those inner feelings of change with nothing concrete to build upon. But it was as though Magician's charisma compelled me to feel that way," Just Middle Manager stated, feeling even less qualified to become Next Great Leader but still wanting to justify his feelings.

Sage could see that this young traveler was teachable but was also still full of doubt. Nevertheless, ignoring the character flaws, Sage spoke strongly about Ruler and Magician.

"Yes, Ruler is known for being rather forceful and objective in the assessment of others and in regard to what needs to be done. But Ruler also gives you great insight into following prescribed rules and procedures. Without Ruler, much damage can be done in life. But a life of Ruler with no Magician can be confining and controlling. If you balance Ruler with the dichotomy of Magician, you can get a real sense of vision and productivity. Magician alone can be manipulating and can generate inappropriate types of outward motivation; for in Magician's bag of tricks there are few, if any, rules. Magician conjures up potions that are not always tested or true. They are mysterious. Some follow them aimlessly, led to follow more by the charisma of the Magician than the power of the potion. But if you balance Magician with Ruler's guidelines, policies, and procedures, you keep the manipulation in check. That is where true potential for others and for projects can come to fruition in real accomplishment. "I am overwhelmed by what you have seen in my journey that I clearly missed," Just Middle Manager responded, relaxing in the small chair for the first time, not really concerned about how his posture looked to Sage.

"You might also consider those you have met in another fashion," Sage continued, not waiting for Just Middle Manager to actually digest their dialogue thus far before continuing. "The four you met in the valley gave you a certain preparation for life. They assisted you in the development of your attitude toward the world around you: Hope, Danger, Warring, or Caring."

"Conversely the four in the forest expanded upon the previous four by shaping those attitudes and providing you with the ability to look within and, therefore, equipping you to adjust your life's journey: Seeking, Loving, Destroying, or Creating."

"If those in the valley taught me to adjust to the outward world around me, and those in the forest to adjust inwardly, what does the harmony of those centered on Celestial City of Influence provide me?" Just Middle Manager asked, now fully leaning forward on the desk and soaking in the wisdom of Sage.

Sage seemed to enjoy the student's change in posture. It appeared as though Just Middle Manager was becoming an astute learner. Sage liked that.

"The last four—Ruler, Magician, *myself*, and he who you will soon meet, Jester—are at the end of your journey because with them, you learn to complete your mission. They assist you in the transformation of the gifts you may have discovered looking inwardly in the forest and applying them to the life you are about to live: to organize, to change, to instruct, or—as you may soon see—to enjoy."

As Just Middle Manager thought through these various coaches, he felt as though he had discovered a real sense of purpose for his journey. Naturally he didn't want to once again open the door for Ego to enter his life. But he did want to share with Sage what he had learned personally. As a result of these encounters and with what Sage had now insightfully provided, Just Middle Manager felt as though he had his own meaning of their connection.

"May I humbly share my thoughts?" he asked, hoping he would impress the professor slightly. But more importantly, he wanted to demonstrate he really deserved to be called Next Great Leader.

"Certainly, you may. What did you witness in this valuable journey you are taking?" Sage asked, wanting to observe what this student may have learned. At the same time, Sage took a large roll of parchment and a quill pen to record what Just Middle Manager was about to utter.

"Well, I didn't observe the coaches in the context of their dichotomies, as you put it, or, as you indicated, in sets of four. I simply viewed them in their whole, for what they taught me about leadership and my desire to discover my leadership style," he began, looking up at Sage.

He noticed that Sage was recording on the roll of parchment each word he spoke. He stopped the dialogue, waiting for Sage to catch up, only resuming when Sage nodded for him to go on.

"I see that in my leadership style I will begin with much hope and vision for those I lead. This I learned from Innocence. I learned to look at my followers with optimism and anticipation of what is good and right. But when working with any group of individuals, I will soon see that there is much danger and difficulty ahead in our journey together. I was taught that lesson as Orphan was pulling me back from the edge of the cliff," Just Middle Manager spoke, looking for some sense of approval from Sage. But it didn't come from any look he might receive, as Sage was still actively and meticulously recording his every word.

Just Middle Manager was hoping Sage was listening to him and not just lost in the work of the parchment. "But as I continued onto the valley floor, it was Warrior and Caregiver who taught me that if I have the discipline of life and war through it, and with a sense of care and concern for others, there are plenty of rewards for us all. It was from them that I learned to be a strong servant-leader, who would fight for others and even help carry their loads if necessary."

"And how exactly do you view the aspect of warring and caring for the group you lead?" Sage asked, not looking up from the parchment with the pen still moving frantically to catch up.

Caught off guard that Sage was actually listening but not confused with the question, Just Middle Manager answered, saying, "Warring is not limited to using just a sword and knife, nor is it complete by lending a helping hand or even acting as a servant by carrying the load of another. Warring can be accomplished by leading those who follow the regular path to leave that path and take a risk in the forest of life. Seeker's passion for exploration showed me that. But to avoid a life of loneliness and constant journey, I must be careful to maintain the bliss and ecstasy of being together and having relationships with others; Lover's home, pictures, and memorabilia inspired such a thought."

"For in keeping the balance between the two, I may avoid leading everyone into a dark forest, only to stand alone. And you, Sage, taught me about that balance."

Upon hearing the last statement, Sage looked up from the writing just briefly to offer a small smile of approval. Just Middle Manager thought the smile was much deeper than Sage was willing to let on.

With the apparent approval from Sage, he continued to talk about the lessons from Destroyer and Creator. "But leading others down a new path, even with the ability to embrace and enmesh with each other, I also learned I must teach others to let go of that which is no longer profitable for them or for the organization. I learned from Destroyer the art of letting go. I learned it with much difficulty, but I learned it," he said, rubbing his leg more for effect than because it was still actually sore.

Sage didn't look up from the work at the desk this time. Just Middle Manager thought he might have overdone the rubbing of the leg. But he knew what he said was the truth. He did learn the lesson with much difficulty and wasn't afraid to say it. The scar from the fall was now a good memory for him.

After a brief delay, Sage asked, "And what did the lesson of Creator and the flooded river teach you about leadership?"

"It was Creator who taught me to not let go without first coming up with new innovative and clever ways to do what we do. But learning that lesson before the fall from the face of the rock would have been better."

"To avoid tragedy and floods of mistakes, it was important that I discovered the need to follow Ruler's procedures, policies, and guidelines. They will keep the new idea from blowing up and causing us to lose our way. It is important to have standards, even if you come across somewhat strict and bossy. The standards of Ruler taught me what can happen if you forsake the burden of leadership for personal comfort or safety."

"And what did you learn to do to balance any extreme of Ruler?" Sage quickly asked.

Without hesitating, Just Middle Manager answered, "Well, to balance those stringent and tight guidelines, I learned to see the potential that is within the group and to use my charisma to bring about a real metamorphic change. Rules don't always apply clearly. Sometimes you have to be able to see beyond them and learn to develop others, even when they don't see the potential themselves. Transformation is in the lives of my followers, I just have to learn how to move them beyond the boundaries of any system and get them to see there is metamorphosis within. This was Magician's gift to me."

"Not surprisingly, I only struggle with the ability to accomplish this, not with *knowing* that I need to do it. For I now know why I learned this lesson and the others. A wonderful friend named Sage enlightened me to these lessons and more," Just Middle Manager added, concluding his review and drawing a much-needed smile of praise from Sage.

As Just Middle Manager finished the summation of the thoughts now contained in his backpack, he felt good about expressing it to someone. He knew the thoughts were still very fluid in his mind, but somehow, he felt as though all the questions he had started out with were starting to find their answers in his encounters with these coaches of life.

He began to think of them as counselors rather than coaches in his life—counselors he could and should call upon when necessary at the proper junctions of life. And from Sage, he had learned that if he was ever stuck in the presence of one coach or counselor too long, or more pointedly, in the shadowy side of their character, he should call upon their dichotomy for help. It would be their opposite that would bring him back to the strength side of that particular coach.

"You have well spoken," Sage said, finally putting the pen down on the table and looking across at Just Middle Manager. "But there remains a certain question for you."

"What is that?" he asked, fearing he had missed the major essay questions on this test.

"What do you say further of me and the fool who is around the last corner? Does Sage play any additional part? And what does Jester add to your journey?"

Just Middle Manager thought for a moment, not really knowing that much about the "fool" around the corner named Jester. But he knew this was who Ruler said was the keeper at the gate of Exuberant Jubilation.

Just Middle Manager thought that Sage was fishing for more praise and adulation and thought it best to deliver it, so he said, "I know little of the person who remains at the last gate of Celestial City of Influence, but I do know that you offer to my backpack much knowledge, wisdom, and sobriety for my leadership. I see now how important it is to analyze and to study, deducting meaning and insights from my experiences. You have taught me to not be delayed by the smaller things of life but to look for both the patterns and the deeper insights."

"And what of my shadowy side," Sage asked, settling back into the large chair and taking a long drag on the pipe. It was obvious it had diminished in flame and fire long ago.

It didn't really appear to Just Middle Manager that Sage thought there was a shadowy side to knowledge, wisdom, and insight, but he thought he would say what he had learned. After all, this is what being a Sage was all about. He might as well practice the newly learned skill in front of a real Sage.

"I fear you may be, at times, rather smug and act somewhat like a know-it-all," he said. The words seemed to come out entirely too fast and too blunt. He wasn't even sure where those thoughts came from, but his deductive reasoning was in full gear, and, having said it, he felt as though he were right.

"You think I am *smug* and a *know-it-all*?" Sage said, the pipe almost falling out as Sage gasped in disbelief.

"No, I don't think you *are* smug, but you can seem that way. Your standing farther up the marble steps and continuing to move higher as I approached made it seem as though you liked a certain position over others. And your overly big desk and chair don't really seem that big unless you compare it with the chair you offered me. You seem to use these objects to put yourself at a position of higher degree."

"And the columns out front are very nice, but they are lined with your own words, wisdom, degrees, and accomplishments. That seems a bit too much for most, I would think," Just Middle Manager answered, trying hard to temper what he saw in his analysis but failing to do so completely. He began to feel that because of his bluntness and critical spirit, he might cloud the lessons he had just diligently proved himself worthy of discovering.

"You have done well, Just Middle Manager," Sage responded, taking the parchment and rolling it carefully. Sage tried to ignore Just Middle Manager's coarse assessment, but the observations made some sense.

Affirming Just Middle Manager's comments, Sage said, "There are many who feel I am this way. I try to hide these things, but I do fall into the trap of seeming more superior to others."

"Perhaps you need someone to balance your nature? Could it be that you need the steadiness of someone who can take your seriousness and your sobriety and blend it into a wonderful concoction of freedom, someone who has a sense of joy and has, perhaps, a little sense of humor?" Just Middle Manager asked, knowing full well who he was referring to.

"Yes, perhaps that is what I need," Sage responded, a slight smile coming across his face. "Now take this parchment on to the person you so describe. I hear you may find such a one at the fourth and final gate of the city. Perhaps there you will receive the seal you need."

"The *seal* I need?" Just Middle Manager asked, jumping off his chair as he saw Sage stand and come out from behind the desk.

"Yes, the seal. You see the words you spoke, and that I recorded on this parchment, are now your right of passage. The transformation you felt with Magician and the knowledge and wisdom you have gleaned here are contained upon the parchment, your personal rite of passage to Celestial City of Influence. But it is not valid without a seal. Once you have the seal, you can return to the gate of Ruler and show your valid documentation."

"So there is documentation I am to have?"

"Of course there is documentation! Ruler would have it no other way. All leaders must show, in this manner, that they are worthy to be leaders. But you can only do so by transforming your experiences into valid knowledgeable and truthful principles by which you can lead. Albeit, you do lack a final seal for your rite of passage, and the only place in the entire city to get the seal is at the fourth gate," Sage said, explaining as they walked along and descended the marble steps together. However, Just Middle Manager couldn't help but notice that Sage waited for him to take a downward step before following suit, always remaining higher than Just Middle Manager. *Perhaps old habits die hard*, he thought.

As Just Middle Manager left the presence of Sage, he noticed how very much alone they had been during their dialogue. The quietness of their discussion was also noticed by Just Middle Manager. With that thought he began to reach the fourth and final corner of Celestial City of Influence, he very much sensed the quietness and soberness surrounding Sage were gone. It was being replaced by the sounds of frivolity and a sense of playfulness.

As he approached the fourth corner, the noise level was almost more than he could bear. The pitch of the singing and joking was more than he had experienced. As he turned the corner, a smile came across his face. He didn't know why, but the joy of those he saw dancing and enjoying life seemed to be contagious even from a far distance.

It wasn't long before he was lost in the music and jubilation. This gate looked like a great place to be. *But what part does this have in my leadership style*, he asked. *What type of seal could I get here*?

As Just Middle Manager stood taking in the entire circus-like atmosphere, he couldn't help but notice that everyone had a smile on their face. Everyone except the fellow walking directly toward him. And he knew who this traveler was. They had met before.

Insight Tips for putting *Leader Sage* to work in your own Leadership Style - *Successfully*

1 Embrace and perfect your ability to analyze and use deductive reasoning. Others may not be as good at it, but you are, and that is a great asset to your leadership style and approach. Fully utilize your ability to gather data and know facts. This only adds to the ability to scrutinize the problem(s).

2 Be careful in your scrutiny that you don't become overly critical of others, alienating their input and contributions. They may not be as equipped as you are to see all the patterns or to know all the issues of the problem. But they do have some things to offer. Take what they give you and build upon it without offending them.

3 You can be superior to others (and possible most others). That comes with its rewards and risks. You can tend to get all the accolades for knowledge and study but still miss out on real friendships and interaction if others think you feel you are too smart or good for them.

4 Try to show your emotional side once in awhile, even if it hurts. Being smart, intellectual, knowledgeable, and/or wise doesn't have to always be stuffy. Learn to laugh at a situation sometimes rather than just getting into analytical or serious mode.

5 Remember, others may be learning things you don't know. Ask them to tell you what they know so that you don't become overly disinterested in smaller things in life. Yes, their stories and experiences might be simple and seemingly unimportant, but they are important to them. You might learn something having listened to the knowledge of others.

Words of Enjoyment and Humor from Leader Jester

"Hello, how are you doing?" Just Middle Manager asked, noticing that not only was there no smile on the face of the traveler coming at him, but the parchment he held in his hand was both wet and torn.

"How am I doing, you ask?" Learner of Much spoke, pushing Just Middle Manager aside and moving back toward the third corner of the city wall. Obviously not happy, he was headed directly toward Sage.

"What happened? Did you obtain your seal?" Just Middle Manager asked, but feared Learner of Much might be too angry or frustrated to converse with him.

Without pause, when the word "seal" was mentioned, Learner of Much stopped in his tracks and turned, angrily, to respond to Just Middle Manager. "My seal, you ask? What good is a seal when the buffoons over there destroyed my entire parchment," Learner of Much spoke, nodding back toward the fourth gate of the city. His voice reached a high peak when he uttered the word *parchment.* Simultaneously, he raised the torn document. It was the same one that Just Middle Manager had dislodged from his hand during their collision earlier on the steps at Sage's gate.

"You are not having much luck with your rite of passage, are you?" Just Middle Manager asked, trying to seem sensitive but, also, pointing out the obvious.

"My luck, sir, is just fine. But I have no desire to go any further with Jester and his merry group."

"But, must you not retrieve a seal from Jester to validate your documentation?" Just Middle Manager asked, showing honest concern for Learner of Much but also wanting to learn something about his own possible encounter with Jester.

"Jester has no idea about a *seal*. Nor do the fools who are engaged in a perpetual party with Jester," Learner of Much added and once again headed for the gate of Sage.

"Perhaps, you can at least tell me what happened, that I might learn from you," Just Middle Manager shouted. He was hoping Learner of Much would give him some insight that he might recognize some pattern or draw some piece of wisdom from him.

Learner of Much stopped his progress one more time and turned to address Just Middle Manager. Walking back to be in a closer proximity, he spoke to Just Middle Manager in a clear but concise tone, much like a mother would who was about to tell her child for the last and final time about the dangers concerning a given situation.

"I simply joined in the party you see occurring over there," he spoke, pointing toward the fourth gate of the city. "I was having a great time with them all, and they seemed to accept me into their group. Then I asked one of them where I could get a seal. That is when a young fool named Enjoyment of All made some stupid remark about going to the ocean, and the others started to bark like the juveniles they are. Enjoyment of All actually got up on the table and started to clap with his hands and bark like a sea lion."

"I know of Enjoyment of All. He was with the group at the first gate, and Ruler sent him on to Jester whereas some others went the other direction to Magician," Just Middle Manager said, recalling the incident of Enjoyment of All's making fun at Ruler's expense. Just Middle Manager could just imagine Enjoyment of All jumping onto a table clapping and barking like a sea lion. But he quickly calmed himself and took a more serious pose when it appeared as though Learner of Much was less indulged by the thought.

"But it was simply a play on words, and Enjoyment of All is an affable traveler. Surely no harm was meant," Just Middle Manager said, trying to ease the moment.

"Yes, I know I am being a little sensitive over a simple joke, but that is not what I am frustrated about," Learner of Much said, admitting that the levity was not all that harsh. "I am frustrated because when Enjoyment of All jumped onto the table and began to clap, he knocked a large amount of liquid over my entire parchment. Now I have to return to Sage and request another. To top it all off, the group gathered there observing the incident and received more laughter out of the spillage and my frustration than any humor from the antics about the seal. I shall not return to these fools, even if Sage does grant my request for a new rite of passage."

With those final words, Learner of Much turned and headed back in the direction of Sage. It wasn't long before he was completely around the corner and in the pursuit of the sober and quiet surroundings Sage offered, along with the desk and the magnificent four columns.

"He will provide you with a new rite of passage, my friend, but you will still need to come to me to obtain your 'seal,'" a voice behind Just Middle Manager spoke.

As Just Middle Manager turned to locate the source of the voice talking behind him, he did so just in time to see a rather short-statured person heading back up the path toward the fourth and final gate of the city. The appearance of the figure reminded Just Middle Manager of a short clown in a large circus. Whereas Magician's gate was full of colors due to the many butterflies gathered about and the robe of Sage was pure white, the clothes on this figure revealed that this had to be Jester. He could have made that assumption by just looking at the multitude of colors Jester wore. But the colors were only background noise to Jester's hat. With bells at the end of each of its three long corners, the hat seemed to sing a song as Jester joined the rest of the group.

There was a small table in the middle of the party, and Jester took a position around it as if to indicate it was the clothes, the hat, and the person of Jester that was at the epicenter of their frivolity.

Just Middle Manager followed Jester to the table and the makeshift control center for fun. He attempted, in spite of the loud noise, to start a conversation with Jester. Since it was impossible to be heard the first time, he repeated his sentence again to Jester, but this time almost screaming, "He was a little upset, I think," referring to Learner of Much.

"You think?" Jester said, not really looking at Just Middle Manager with the response but instead taking another drink of a beverage seemingly belonging to no one, abandoned on the table. Jester seemed to be lost in the commotion and frivolity of those dancing and singing around him.

Just Middle Manager wasn't sure Jester even noticed him or heard what he said.

Just Middle Manager sat at the table across from Jester for a moment, feeling unusually awkward and out of place. But as the music began to decline in volume, he thought he might as well ask about the seal and then perhaps make his way toward Ruler. Just Middle Manager was not very gregarious, and the loudness at this gate was a little more than he liked. His thought was to get the seal, whatever it was, and then get back to the seriousness of entering Celestial City of Influence.

But, before he could say anything, Jester ceased observation of the crowd and spoke to him first, "I am Jester, and you must be Just Middle Manager?"

Insight: The appetite of a leader following the style of Leader Jester is about having a great time and seeking enjoyment in life. The Jester sees enjoyment in almost all situations. A Jester may view others as either sources of humor or, perhaps, those who he or she can play a joke on or have fun with. The Jester's desire to find enjoyment and to be playful motivates their behaviors. Leader Jester will inspire those they lead to seek fun and fulfillment of life through enjoyment, rewarding those who are a joy to be around or who find a way to make life fun and enjoyable for others. At the end of the day, the Jester might say it was a great day because they had fun and made others laugh.

"Well, I am. But how did you kn—"

"Yes, I know who you are and where you're traveling and even why you're traveling. Just because I am wearing a crazy hat doesn't mean I don't know anything. Why don't we get you a drink? And you look like you haven't eaten in a long time. Let's get you some food. It is always more fun to have these conversations with food in your stomach and with a beverage in your hand."

"Well, I haven't eaten in a long time, but I would prefer to just get to work and to secure what I came for," Just Middle Manager said, lowering his voice as to not become the butt of someone's joke or fun.

"You don't seem to enjoy life much, do you?" Jester asked, returning to gaze at the revelers surrounding the Gate of Exuberant Jubilation. "Tell me, what do you see?"

"I see a lot of people having a party," Just Middle Manager answered, only briefly gazing about before uttering his reply. Yet, if all these travelers were preparing to be Next Great Leader, he actually thought he saw a lot of wasted energy and lack of focus. But he didn't want to say such a thing to someone named Jester.

Insight: Jester enjoys discussion and problem solving in a nonthreatening and fun environment. They may often suggest moving a difficult discussion to a place of fun and enjoyment. Food is a great ally to the Jester, not because the food is magical, but the consumption of food is often accompanied by fun and enjoyment. They may also problem solve on a basketball court, play tennis, or any environment that allows them to surround the problem with play. However, because of this approach to life and problems, the Jester is not always taken seriously. The plot of their lives acts as a two-edged sword for them. On one edge, they get the advantage of alleviating stress with levity, but on the other side, they are often dismissed as the clowns they pretend to be.

"After spending all that time with Sage, that is the best analysis you can muster," Jester said with a long and loud laugh. "You hope to be Next Great Leader, and all you see here is people having a party?"

"What else is there to see, Jester?" Just Middle Manager asked as he began taking a more serious look at the group.

He could make out Enjoyment of All but really wasn't sure what he was doing. He was still on top of the table, but it didn't appear as though he were dancing.

"There, that individual over there on the table," Jester spoke, pointing to the same person who had caught Just Middle Manager's eye.

"You mean Enjoyment of All?" Just Middle Manager asked, but added quickly so as to not actually be associated with such an odd person, "I met him at the gate of Ruler. That is my only familiarity with him."

"That's too bad. He really knows how to enjoy life," Jester said, taking a full pull of his drink and almost laughing out loud at Enjoyment of All, who was now off the table but acting like he was either on fire or been stung by a swarm of bees.

"That is 'enjoyment of life'?" Just Middle Manager asked, worrying that he would never really enjoy life if that was the case.

"What do you think Enjoyment of All is doing over there?" Jester asked, a smile and laughter carrying each word.

Just Middle Manager didn't really want to say what he thought of Enjoyment of All. He had already heard the foolishness of the traveler at the Gate of Structured Discipline. Ruler didn't seem to have much use for Enjoyment of All, and Just Middle Manager didn't think Sage would either. The bias of his answer would be obvious, but he had learned from Sage to scrutinize and to discover patterns. The pattern he had didn't say much good about Enjoyment of All.

"I think he is wasting his time on enjoyment, and he will never really be Next Great Leader. He has a difficult time being serious about life," Just Middle Manager said, making a true statement to how he felt but not really saying it in the manner he wished.

"That is blunt!" Jester responded and then rose from the table. "If it is your seal you desire, relax," Jester said as he began to walk away, almost ignoring Just Middle Manager's bluntness. "But first, we enjoy, then we talk business," Jester said and then headed toward a room off to the side and away from the major merrymaking.

Halfway to the room, Jester noticed that Just Middle Manager was not following. Gesturing for him to follow along, Jester stopped to listen to a discussion some were having under a gazebo to the left of the city gate.

"I think they are entirely worried for no reason and are acting much too serious about the whole thing," Grasper of Life spoke and then noticed Jester standing near the gazebo. "What do you think, Jester?"

"Well, you just used the word *serious* in that sentence. I prefer to not have my name mentioned that closely to such an archaic word," Jester said, again with a laugh and a smile.

Just Middle Manager caught up with Jester just in time to hear a loud and long laugh come from the many that had squeezed under the makeshift porch. He wasn't sure what the laughter was about, but those who were there knew. They seemed to be captivated with Jester.

Insight: Others will turn to Jester for leadership, but he or she may shy away from such responsibility, either because they have little confidence in their ability or because they don't want to lose their persona of being fun to be around. The prototypical leadership model doesn't work for the Jester, as it is too confining and too full-time serious. They may attempt to lead, however, by getting others to do the work or tricking others into carrying the load.

"You seem to bring out the laughter and joy in others," Just Middle Manager said, following Jester into a room. The nameplate on the door read "Jester's Office: No Work, All Play." The room looked more like a young person's playroom than a working environment. Each table in the room was well-equipped to host multiple game activities. Despite numerous tables, there were no signs of an actual workspace. If there was work going on, it was hidden by the game-like atmosphere and paraphernalia.

Upon entry to the room, Jester collected two black and white stones laying on one of the tables and rolled them across the surface. The stones were cut in a square-like fashion with black and white sides alternating with each other. The stones came to halt on the table with two black sides looking up at Jester.

"It's going to be a rough day," Jester said, tossing the stones back into a dirty cup poised on the table.

"What do you mean 'It's going to be a rough day'?" Just Middle Manager asked, taking a seat in an overstuffed chair that looked like it had been decorated with sauce from Jester's favorite food.

"It is just a little game I play," Jester answered. "If I come in the door and the stones roll white face up, it will be a good day. But, if they roll black face up like that, it is going to be a rough workday."

"This is where you work?" Just Middle Manager asked, ignoring Jester's juvenile approach to workday evaluations. "It looks more like a playroom than a workroom."

"There you go again, showing off your lack of ability to have fun and your obvious disdain for life's little pleasures," Jester commented and took a seat in a chair that was shaped in the form of an animal.

Insight: Jesters will often create a workspace where play is the main décor and fun the featured centerpiece. The conclusion may be that it would be difficult to carry on serious work in such a locale, but the real enterprise of Jester is to do exactly that: Carry on serious work in a non-serious environment and, therefore, making work fun and the experience of it electrifying.

"I don't disdain life's pleasures!" Just Middle Manager said, realizing he hadn't spent a lot of time in his life actually evaluating that thought.

"You may not disdain life's pleasures, but you certainly don't notice or embrace them," Jester said, looking over some papers that were on the table.

"What do you mean I don't notice them?" Just Middle Manager responded, trying to think about the most recent observation he had made. He did notice all those singing and dancing outside. *What else was there to notice,* he thought.

Jester returned the papers to the table, doing nothing with them, and then said to Just Middle Manager, "What did you notice about the pleasures and enjoyment of your travel thus far?"

Just Middle Manager was taken aback by the question. He had certainly observed the party atmosphere at the fourth gate and those who had engaged with Jester around the gazebo. He had also remembered and noticed Enjoyment of All, both at Ruler's gate and dancing on the table just outside the room. But he had to admit he hadn't taken much time to enjoy his journey, mostly because he was so occupied with the heaviness of his backpack and the seriousness of his mission.

Observing Just Middle Manager's pensive behavior, Jester made a half-hearted excuse to leave the room and returned in a few moments with a notepad and pen. Turning to Just Middle Manager, Jester said, "Let's play a game. I will give you five minutes for you to record for me all the things you enjoyed about your journey to Celestial City of Influence. If you get the assignment done, I will buy you dinner. If you don't, you buy me dinner."

Taking the notepad and pen, Just Middle Manager simply stared at the blank sheets and into blank space. Now that he was confronted with the thought, he realized that he hadn't given himself much time to enjoy anything. That thought seemed to overwhelm him.

Insight: Jesters enjoy turning work into a playful game that allows them to find a pleasurable outcome at the end. They may, at times, however, annoy others since every task is surrounded with a gimmick or trick. They may get drained of energy by simply going into a simple work mode for too long of a time period.

"I can't seem to recall anything in particular," he said, not really wanting to admit to Jester that he didn't really have any memories of enjoyment over the past journey. "Is there something in particular I am supposed to recall?"

"I have no idea; it is your journey."

"Well, I have no thought. This was not a vacation adventure. I was on a serious undertaking to discover my leadership style and to qualify myself as Next Great Leader. I really wasn't on a holiday. Do you understand?"

"Yes, I understand. You were so actively engaged in the pursuit of your goals that you had little or no time to notice any enjoyment, fun, or humor during that pursuit."

"You make it sound so serious and so sad." Just Middle Manager put his head down, not looking at Jester.

"I simply repeated what you said. You said you were on a serious journey," Jester said, seemingly finding some enjoyment in the banter since a smile was seen coming across the pleasantly plump face.

"What do you see that is so humorous?" Just Middle Manager asked, annoyed Jester would find humor about what he thought was a serious and sound mission of life.

"I find *you* humorous!" Jester said. This time, fortunately, the tone in Jester's voice seemed to finally find some gravitas. "For someone who is taking such a serious journey of life, it would seem to me you would desire to reap some enjoyment from it as well as knowledge, insights, and wisdom. You seem to be so wrapped up in your quest, you forgot perhaps one of the most important aspects of life and living, much less of leading—enjoyment!"

"How do leading *and* enjoyment find harmony?" Just Middle Manager asked, already realizing that if you can't enjoy something, it would be a miserable occupation to serve each day.

"Leadership is serious, yes, but there is life to be lived and enjoyment to be had. Take this fellow out there, Enjoyment of All. You probably thought he was just wasting his time and not really engaged in any type of work or sound productivity."

"You are correct," Just Middle Manager said. "He looks like he is just wasting away his life."

"I would agree he does lack some in leadership. Since he has not yet traveled to Magician or Sage's gate, he has much to learn to transform himself into a great leader. But did you notice the audience he was dancing for?" Jester asked, leaning slightly forwarded in the chair as he turned around and mounted backward.

"No, I only noticed Enjoyment of All."

"Well, if you would have noticed the audience, your opinion of him might have changed. We are not having a party out there in the courtyard. We are entertaining several very ill adventurers who have traveled to our city for one reason, their life is ending and they wish to find pleasure in the finality of their days."

Set back by the seriousness of the thought, Just Middle

Manager asked, "If they are so ill, shouldn't something be done for them? Shouldn't we discover some cure or create a place for them to be comfortable? Perhaps they should be brought to Sage, who may find a secret cure for their illness."

"Have you ever talked to someone whose life is ending?" Jester asked, and then before Just Middle Manager could answer, stated, "Haven't you noticed that those whose lives are soon to end give those of us who are still full of life the same advice over and over: 'Enjoy your life while you have it to live.' People want enjoyment out of life. Even in leadership, you must find a way to have fun and convert the most serious moments from their negative energy into positive enjoyment. People actually work harder and more productively when they are enjoying their vocation. Take those involved in athletic competition. They work harder than most at a discipline simply because they take pleasure in their game. Leadership must get others to get the job done, but to do so at the expense of pleasure is not leadership but tyranny."

As they continued their discussion over the bread and wine Jester had delivered to the room, Just Middle Manager paid for it because the five minutes to write something he enjoyed about his trip had expired. He was hoping Jester was kidding, but there was no humor in the bet.

It wasn't long before Just Middle Manager was actually laughing and enjoying himself. He laughed the loudest when he recalled Warrior poking at the bushes with his sword. Jester laughed the loudest when told about Orphan pulling Just Middle Manager from falling over a cliff and then even louder when hearing about him letting go of the rope ladder too soon and falling with a thud at the feet of Destroyer. They both thought the sight of him sitting on a rock in the middle of Creator's river explosion was extremely humorous.

With those long and loud laughs at his expense, however, Just Middle Manager thought he would ask the obvious question: "Don't you think, because of your humor and the bent for play in life, you take the risk of hurting someone's feelings or even alienating them from your insights?"

"There are many who cannot adapt to my humor; that is true," Jester conceded. "Take a look at Learner of Much, who has left us and is now engaged once again in full conversation with Sage. He longs for sobriety and is overly offended at humor."

"The inability of others to find enjoyment in life is not a reason for me to forego my own. Too many people gripped by the tentacles of sobriety miss out on the littlest pleasures of simple merriment. They rent entirely too many rooms in their mind to soberness. I, my friend, prefer to lease a couple of choice locations for fun and humor. There was a very wise man named Solomon who said, 'Laughter is good medicine.' And I intend on sharing that particular drug with as many leaders as I can."

"Solomon, you say? That is funny. Sage quoted the same fellow," Just Middle Manager said, finishing off the tall glass of wine before him.

"Sage does well to quote such a wise person, and so do I. Perhaps this wise fellow teaches you that wisdom and humor are closer than you think, Just Middle Manager?"

The two finished the bottle of wine, the bread, and their discussion. They agreed like all the others that Jester had a shadowy side. Some would think there was no seriousness to Jester, or when Jester was working and playing, others might think there was too much of one and not enough of the other.

Jester decided this is something most jesters would just have to live with. Jester decided to simply pursue a vision for excellence with enjoyment and to let others determine if there was work or play being completed. To Jester, it would always be both simultaneously.

"But you came to me for something did you not?" Jester said, standing and walking back to the table and retrieving the papers once held.

"Yes, I need a seal for my rite of passage. But I am not sure what the seal is or what it is for," Just Middle Manager said, following Jester toward the table. In the process, however, he tripped over a small ball that was left on the floor of the room, landing awkwardly on the same leg he injured when he fell off the face of the cliff with a thud at Destroyer's feet. But before Jester could offer an apology, Just Middle Manager began to laugh. Unlike the first time he fell, Just Middle Manager found some humor in his pain.

Just Middle Manager rehearsed, again, the account of his fall off Destroyer's ladder. They both laughed for a brief moment, and then Jester explained the seal and its purpose. In most royal courts the jester had the ability to say almost anything he or she wanted to in the king's presence. A good jester could even insult the king if done with the proper humor and sarcasm. That gave the jester significant powers in the royal court. Others would often come to the jester and encourage them to say one thing or another in the king's ear. A good jester would be one who could balance the severity of their comments with the humor of their life.

Therefore, Jester explained that when the seal was applied to the outside of the parchment, it would allow Ruler to see that Just Middle Manager had his rite of passage. It showed he had qualified his journey in the presence of Magician and Sage. It also verified that Just Middle Manager had discovered the balance of leadership and humor from Jester. The seal would speak the language of Ruler.

Looking at the seal and the parchment in his hand, Just Middle Manager made his way through the crowd and toward the first gate of the city, the gate of Structured Direction. As he passed by Enjoyment of All, he noticed a sickly and weak-looking fellow in a chair, laughing. Enjoyment of All had actually taken a bucket and placed it on his head. The seated traveler was actually having trouble breathing because he was laughing so hard.

"You are doing a great job there, Enjoyment of All. I really like your enthusiasm and sense of humor," Just Middle Manager said, feeling as awkward as the statement actually sounded.

"Do I know you?" Enjoyment of All asked, not stopping the dance since this audience of one was fully captivated and engaged in laughter.

"No, I only observe your behavior and desire to obtain some

of it for myself," Just Middle Manager said, not really thinking he could.

"Well, grab a bucket and join in my friend."

Now typically, Just Middle Manager would simply pass by and give a polite smile. Especially since he had his rite of passage with Jester's seal to demonstrate he had struck a proper balance. But this time he decided to dance. He wasn't sure if it was the wine or the sudden fondness for enjoying his journey, but Just Middle Manager danced through the night. He and Enjoyment of All made not only this dear soul laugh for a brief moment in life but many others as well. They actually made some people laugh who were simply there to observe and had a long life in front of them. Just Middle Manager came to an even deeper understanding of the power of humor and the energy gained from simply enjoying life.

Having danced the night away, Just Middle Manager finally made his leave of them all. He headed toward Ruler's gate to present his rite of passage and seal of approval. He knew he was a transformed person and had now finished his mission. He only had to present his documentation to Ruler and then enter Celestial City of Influence. Soon, Great Leader would be renaming him Next Great Leader. A smile came across his face as he left Jester's gate.

Jester watched Just Middle Manager depart and sat back at the table in the center of the party. A smile came across Jester's face as Just Middle Manager said goodbye to those he had danced with all night and as he returned to Ruler's gate.

This fellow seemed to have learned all the right lessons and balanced them in all the right ways. But would he become Next Great Leader? Jester didn't know the answer, but he knew how hard the interview with Great Leader would be. Was Just Middle Manager up for that one question from Great Leader?

Insight Tips for putting *Leader Jester* to work in your own Leadership Style - *Successfully*

1	Keep your sense of humor. Don't allow others to rent "serious" space in your entire mind. If they attempt to, write them a "serious" eviction notice. Your energy is your humor, and without it you are not you.
2	Remember that others are not always in tune to your humor. They may observe and believe that your enjoyment of life is not warranted and not proper behavior to have in a work setting. You may have to temper what you do, or more importantly, educate them as to why you are trying to mix work with play.
3	Work and play don't always mix well. You can't always go to the bar or have a company picnic to solve confrontations or complex problems. However, you can find a way to mix them if you are finding a balance between sobriety and levity. Too much of either is never good. They mix better if they have an equal proportion.
4	Be careful that in your quest for fun and humor you don't hurt others. Sometimes your humor is taken the wrong way, and people's feelings are hurt. Temper your humor with a desire to be courteous and caring.
5	Be aware that a constantly funny person is great to have in the break room but not always welcome in the boardroom or the war room. If you want to be followed and to have influence on others, you have to learn to turn off the humor until you are able to establish a more appropriate setting to let it fly.

Part III:

Conclusion

Next Great Leader or Still Just Middle Manager?

Just Middle Manager took several large breaths into his lungs as he stood before the gate. His journey had come to fruition, and he was excited about the prospects beyond this entry.

Although Ruler had been very busy directing and organizing others at the Gate of Structured Direction, Just Middle Manager was eventually able to present his documentation and obtain passage into Celestial City of Influence. This was a marvelous day in his life, and Just Middle Manager could hardly wait. Before he opened the large city gate, he turned one last time to look back toward Follower Village and the path he had taken.

He could see in the far, far distance the small town he had left with such a large pack of questions strapped to his back (the pack now felt not only light on his shoulders but buoyant, almost carrying him into the city). Others from Follower Village were not as eager to see him go and didn't offer much help. They were too busy trying to quench their own hunger than to assist him with his appetite for leadership.

As he caught a glimpse of the sunlight coming up over the valley, he knew his friends Innocent, Orphan, Warrior, and Caregiver lived there and were even now preparing the attitudes of others who would dare to make this trek. That thought comforted him that they too would have great coaches along their journey. *But will they all listen to them*, he asked himself.

Even though the forest was dark and well hidden from his view, Just Middle Manager knew that Seeker and Lover were even now preparing a weary traveler to look within and to make choices as to the specific actions for their journey. Would they seek new ways? Would they hold on to the ecstasy they found? Or would they find that necessary balance between the two and choose wisely?

Destroyer and Creator would not fail to add to their voyage, giving him or her much pause about letting go and creating new innovation and ideas. Just Middle Manager hoped whoever followed after him would find a way to let go without falling like a stone and to cross the river without having to go from rock to rock.

As Just Middle Manager watched Ruler (now only a few yards behind him) organize and instruct others, he had to laugh. The first time he had met Ruler he was in envy of that kind of skill of leadership and organization. Magician, Sage, and certainly Jester had given him a balance in life. And whereas he still saw the skill of Ruler, he also found a more evenhanded sense of purpose and excellence for this final stage of his journey.

All of these friends, these counselors, and these coaches, would be necessary in his life if he were to become Next Great Leader. But first, he had to open the gate. He simply had to open the gate ... open the gate ...

"Open them! Roy! Come on, open your eyes. You better hurry. You have an interview this morning, and you're not going to be able to do it with your eyes closed," Jill said. It was the fourth time she had attempted to wake Roy. She had been awake for a while and was now sitting on the bed looking at him with a bowl of Captain Crunch in her hands.

"What? What's going on? Ruler?" Roy asked as he sat up in bed. Rubbing his eyes, he struggled to orient himself. When he did, he could make out Jill, cereal bowl in hand, sitting directly in front of him. There was no Great Leader behind a much desired gate to see him. Jester, Ruler, and the others had vanished as dreams often do, quenched by the light of the morning sun.

"Ruler? What are you talking about?" Jill asked. "You did get the 'ruler' part right. That's me," Jill said, jumping off the bed and heading for the kitchen. "You better hurry up. It's seven-thirty, and you have an interview at Brisco Chemical at nine."

"Seven-thirty? How could you let me sleep so late?" Roy said, bounding out of bed and taking a brief look at the clock on the night stand. As he did, he could see his empty legal pad still laying next to the alarm. It was yet to be written upon.

Calling back on her way to the kitchen (she was set on retrieving some orange juice to wash down her cereal), Jill yelled back, "I didn't let you sleep in. I tried to get you to wake up, but you said something about 'dancing with a bucket on your head' and then went back to sleep. Sounds like you experienced the dream of dreams, Just Middle Manager."

Rushing down the hall to catch up with Jill, Roy shouted, "Wait. Why did you call me that?"

"Call you what?" Jill asked, taking a drink of orange juice directly from a cardboard jug.

"'Just Middle Manager.' Why did you call me 'Just Middle Manager'?"

Jill looked at him rather oddly. "You don't remember our conversation before we went to bed last night? You were all worried about this interview today and wanted to figure out your leadership style so you wouldn't always be just a middle manager. You said you wanted to be a great leader. I think we had a bet, if I remember correctly. We were racing to see who would discover their ... what did we call it ... appetite. But, I won. It was Captain Crunch cereal," Jill said, setting the orange juice jug down and holding up the now almost empty bowl of sugary cereal. "I was hungry for Captain Crunch. It was about four in the morning, but at least I found out what I was hungry for," Jill said. "About that time you were saying something in your sleep about not wanting to let go of a ladder. Then you made a big grunt and fell back to sleep. I am not sure what there was to let go of at four in the morning, but I know you better hurry now. And I hope you discovered your own appetite for leadership!"

"Oh, I have. I don't have time to tell you, but I more than discovered my appetite for my leadership style. I discovered all twelve of them."

Jill just looked at him with a puzzled look and opened up the pantry.

As Roy returned to get ready for his interview, Jill could see him noticeably limping up the narrow hall to their bathroom and asked, "Why are you limping?"

Roy just smiled and called back, "I think I have a cramp in my leg. It's from letting go too soon, or from stepping on a ball."

Jill didn't know what he meant about letting go, but it didn't bother her. She was looking at her discovery within the pantry. There was another Hershey bar staring her right in the face.

As Roy approached the interview room, he was full of excitement and energy. He had met with Sandy and Jim in the break room, and they were shocked at how jovial he was and how much energy he had. Roy tried to explain to them about the dream, but it came off sounding childish and foolish. Jim made a joke about it, and Roy actually laughed. Sandy thought that was unusual as she had never heard Roy actually laugh at work.

Both Jim and Sandy were confused thoroughly by Roy's sudden interest in the leadership styles of the twelve members of the interview committee. But his questions made them believe he simply wanted to know as much as he could about each of the twelve before he entered the interview.

As he pushed open the door to the interview room, he could see that those interviewing him were all seated behind a very long and large table. There was one single chair in front of them all. Harvey Brisco, the president and cofounder of Brisco Chemical, instructed him to sit down in that chair. Brisco was seated in a very large chair in the center of the twelve.

As Roy walked over to the small chair, he did so with a slight limp. He didn't think anyone would notice. But it acted like a scar in his life, something to keep him humble and content.

As he sat in the small chair in front of them all, he said, "Well, this is a nice chair." *It's a little small,* he thought. Sage *would be pleased that I felt comfortable in the room, even sitting in such an intimidating posture and position.*

Mr. Brisco opened the file that was in front of him and was about to say something when Roy spoke first, "Mr. Brisco, thank you for giving me the opportunity to possibly be the next supervisor of Brisco Chemical. I understand you have a question for me, and I would like to answer it by saying—"

"Don't you think I should ask you the question first?" Mr. Brisco interrupted.

Although he didn't say it in a humorous fashion, one of the twelve on the interview committee felt a sudden rush of humor, laughing completely out loud. Roy looked over and saw that although everyone else was a little embarrassed, Pauline from accounting wasn't and made eye contact with Roy. The two of them seemed to know that this was a jester moment, and they decided to enjoy it no matter how brief it may be. Roy knew he and Pauline were on the same wave length, one jester to another.

Casting a disapproving glance in the direction of Pauline, Mr. Brisco went on, saying, "We have certain procedures and guidelines to follow here, and it is best to follow them. Do you agree, Roy?"

"Yes, I do agree, Mr. Brisco," Roy said, and then taking a large breath added, "But, I do think we have to make sure that procedures and policies are balanced by our desire to see change and a metamorphosis takes place in our organization. We have a great place here at Brisco; we have hope and security for the future. But that has to be balanced by our vigilance for dangers and the possibility that our hope might lead us over a well-hidden cliff. But, if, with discipline and ..."

Roy continued to expound about the leadership style he thought Brisco Chemical needed from his future role. He rehearsed for Mr. Brisco the very important role of the ruler. But he was quick to add—speaking more to Philip, who sat on the committee and was from the sales department—that they also needed to adapt to the customer's needs and draw out the butterfly moments of change within the organization. As he spoke, he addressed each of the twelve leaders on the committee and spoke their language and to their appetite, speaking specifically to their individual leadership style. As they listened, they all came to the same conclusion. Mr. Brisco was about to come to the same conclusion.

At the end of the interview, Mr. Brisco turned to the other eleven members of the committee and said, "Folks, Roy may be just a middle manager in our organization, but I think we have found our Next Great Leader!"

Addendum Examples: Following Natural Impulses

The Situation of the Spilled Coffee

Archetype: Each archetype within the organization observes David walking through the work area of the organization, carrying a cup of very hot coffee. David trips, stumbles, and spills the hot coffee down the front of his dress shirt and tie. Each archetype might naturally have the following impulsive response based upon their archetype:

Innocent: "It will be okay. You will see. Once we get it all cleaned up, the day will still be great."

Orphan: "You should have seen that bump in the rug or got a cover for the cup before you took off with the coffee."

Warrior: "I'll help. I can get this cleaned up for you. I will wipe you clean. I almost caught you before you stumbled further."

Caregiver: "Are you okay? Is there anything you need? Would like a new cup of coffee? A new shirt or tie? Do you need to go to the hospital?"

Seeker: "Every journey has its risk. Don't look on this as a bad thing. You now know the way not to carry your coffee!"

Lover: "Don't worry about it; I still think you're a great person. I know it might have been embarrassing, but I am still on your side; and even if others think you are clumsy, this will not damage our relationship."

Destroyer: "Forget about it, and move on. So you spilled coffee. Don't cry over spilled milk, as they say."

Creator: "We should invent something that goes over coffee. So you can transport it without spillage. Or, maybe, we can create a better way to walk through the office, an alternate path, so it doesn't create these hazards."

Ruler: "Did you follow the policy? Are you supposed to have coffee in the work area? Let's make sure we don't have to fill out an accident report."

Magician: "How can we use this incident to change the way you walk or carry things? Can this incident be a defining moment in your life so you can use it to transform the way people should view you rather than how they currently view you?"

Sage: "There are many who spill things while walking. You should note that coffee spills in the office are not unusual. Many have suffered severe burns as a result. The loss of work time due to accidents like this, then again, is marginal."

Jester: "That was great! Wait until I tell the guys in the breakroom. Do you have a second act you do, or was this the main attraction? Do you walk much?"

The Situation of the Loss of Money and Time

Archetype: Each archetype within the organization learns that David has made a large mistake and cost the organization time and money. Each archetype might naturally have the following impulsive response based upon their archetype:

Innocent: "It will be okay. You will see. We can make this work. There are better days ahead. I am sure he didn't mean to do it. He's such a nice guy."

Orphan: "I knew this would happen. We need to make sure this doesn't happen again by having the safeguards in place I warned you all about earlier."

Warrior: "Let me fix it. Show me where the mistake was, and I can figure a way to get us out of it. Let's roll up our sleeves and get this corrected."

Caregiver: "David, are you okay? I am sure you are hurting right now. Do you have some other things that need to be done so you will have more time to devote to this issue? Just let me know what you want me to do."

Seeker: "Let's look at what we have here that can be learned. Is this maybe sending us, as an organization, into a new direction? Are there some options here we haven't considered to solve the issue?"

Lover: "David, I know you hurt, but this will not damage our relationship. We all will just have to hold on and band together. We are going to have to lock arms and become as one. The team will get us through this."

Destroyer: "Let's not dwell on this. If he can't handle the job, then let him go. If he can and made a mistake, then just let it go. We have to get past the blame of it and cut our losses here."

Creator: "Let's look at the current resources we have and put them to work for us. Maybe we can get some lemonade out of this lemon. Is there a way we can take some of the projects we are working on and divert some time and money away from them onto this issue?"

Ruler: "How did this happen? Who was supposed to be watching him to make sure the checks and balances were in place? There are policies to be followed, and if he followed them, this wouldn't have happened. Do we need to put a new policy in place to protect us from this type of thing happening again?"

Magician: "I think David is salvageable. We just need to take some of the things he has done and convert them to positive energy for him and for us. He has some great qualities that maybe we're not using to their fullest. Maybe we put him in the wrong place for his gifts?"

Sage: "If you are going to have an organization, you are going to have mistakes. Let's remember, statistics will tell us that if we hire a better quality of employee, we might avoid some of the minor mistakes. We could send him to a school to reeducate him on his job."

Jester: "Let's just relax. Not all is lost. We still have the company bowling team headed for the finals. I know it is serious, but get real. We can make more money. Let's go to the bar and talk about how to solve it. Or, maybe a company picnic will get our minds off the problem and help us to relax and have some fun."

The Situation of the Layoffs and Cutbacks

Archetype: Each archetype is told there are going to be layoffs and cutbacks within the organization without being told who. Each archetype might naturally have the following impulsive response based upon their archetype:

Innocent: "This can't last forever. We can get through this. Before we know it, we will be on the other side and wonder why we thought it was so tough."

Orphan: "We need to band together and form a coalition. We have to make sure we protect our turf so they go after another department. I knew this would happen if we didn't protect ourselves. Let's make sure we don't get blindsided by something here."

Warrior: "Maybe I can redirect my department to cut back. I can get them to do some extra work, stay longer, and work harder. I won't let the organization down, and I'll find a way to save these jobs."

Caregiver: "What can we do to help out? I know they don't want to hurt anyone. Maybe we can find a way to just help each other out. And if someone is cut, maybe we can all find a way to help that person out during the tough times. We can go over to their home and support them through this rough patch."

Seeker: "This gives us a great chance to find a new way to do business. Let's not look at the old ways of doing things here and try to save what is obviously not working. Maybe we can find a way out of this no one else has seen before."

Lover: "I don't like the idea of breaking up the team. We have been through so much. This team will find a way to pull everyone through it all. We all mean so much to each other and to lose one is to damage us all."

Destroyer: "Let's see who is not pulling their weight around here and let them go first. And if there is a department, project, or system that needs to go, let it go. We are too fat, and it is time for us to cut some of the dead weight."

Creator: "Don't just look at the problem. Let's open our eyes and try to see some vision we haven't seen before. Maybe we can create a new product or new service that will enable us to solve the current crisis. The solution is only a step away if we get creative."

Ruler: "The systems simply need to be followed. We created the current dilemma with our rules, policies, and procedures, and we simply have to revise them to get us out of it. If someone isn't fitting into the system, let's find out why, and that may have to determine which department or staff member needs to go."

Magician: "This is a great chance for us to reinvent ourselves. We have potential here to become something even greater. If someone gets laid off, let's assign them a coordinator that will help them discover something new they can be good at to become even stronger."

Sage: "Think through what we have here. We went through cutbacks twenty years ago, and we survived. We need to make sure our intellectual resources are saved foremost. We need to make sure those who hold the information and knowledge are kept from harm."

Jester: "Oh well. We can always find jobs with the competitor. Or, we could go out and get drunk and just wait to see what will happen. Let's have a company party to relieve the stress. Maybe we could all get together after work for drinks and put our heads together."

How Each Archetype Might Use the Word Help

Archetype: Each archetype might use the word "help" in a sentence in the following way:

Innocent: "Help is on the way!"
Orphan: "God helps those who help themselves!"
Warrior: "Get out of the way, and let me help!"
Caregiver: "Can I help you?"
Seeker: "Let's look for help in other places!"
Lover: "I love the way everyone helps each other around here!"
Destroyer: "I don't need your help anymore!"
Creator: "I have made this thing to help us!"
Ruler: "If you need help, look in the employee manual first!"
Magician: "All the help you need is within you!"
Sage: "Know what you're talking about if you want to help!"
Jester: "If you want help, I'll be at the bar!"

Addendum: Take the Pearson-Marr Archetype Indicator® On-line

The following is taken from the Center for Application of Psychological Type Website and gives you both background and the website to take an on-line version of the Pearson-Marr Archetype Indicator® (PMAI™).

> The Pearson-Marr Archetype Indicator® (PMAI™)
>
> Much of the world knows the work of Carl Jung on psychological type through the *Myers-Briggs Type Indicator®* instrument. Jung's other great contribution to human understanding is the concept of the archetype—the shared myths, themes, images, characters, patterns, and symbols present in our lives and our culture.
>
> The PMAI™, or *Pearson-Marr Archetype Indicator®*, the world's first scientifically validated archetype assessment tool, does for archetypes what the MBTI® instrument does for psychological type. The PMAI and its accompanying guidebook, *Introduction to Archetypes,* open a window into unconscious archetypes and a path to self-understanding.
>
> The assessment is available online at www.capt.org.

The author is not affiliated with or contracted by the Center for Application of Psychological Type and simply offers the above information to further the reader's experience and knowledge of the world of archetypes.

Further Information

www.hulingsandassociates.com

About the Author

After spending time in the military as a trainer for the U.S. Army and in the ministry as both a youth pastor and a senior pastor, David J. Hulings has spent the last twenty years as a motivational performance coach. His one-on-one coaching of business executives and K-12 school administrators has given him many insights and experiences from which to draw practical lessons and leadership principles. As a gifted motivational speaker, Mr. Hulings both educates and entertains his audiences with a story-like delivery that is at the heart of *Just Middle Manager: Next Great Leader.* David lives with his wife, Robin, on their boat, Knotta Shore Thing, in Grand Haven, Michigan.

www.hulingsandassociates.com

CPSIA information can be obtained
at www.ICGtesting.com
Printed in the USA
BVHW042221060220
571676BV00007B/36